Roots of the 1969

WOODSTOCK FESTIVAL

The Backstory to "Woodstock"

Roots of the 1969

WOODSTOCK FESTIVAL

The Backstory to "Woodstock"

Edited by **Weston Blelock**
Julia Blelock

Foreword by Bob Fass

FRONT COVER
Bob Dylan and John Sebastian leave the Café Espresso in Woodstock
on Bob's Triumph motorcycle, 1964. Photo by Douglas R. Gilbert.

OVERLEAF
The Woodstock Village Green in July 1969—a little over a month
before the festival in Bethel. The cultural clash between authority,
youthful rebellion and traditional ways is evoked through the
juxtaposition of the constable, the Mustang convertible full of
kids and the Dutch Reformed Church across the way.
Photo by Edward Hausner; courtesy of the New York Times/Redux.

Related titles available from WoodstockArts:
Woodstock History and Hearsay (second "art book" edition)
It Happened in Woodstock

© 2009 by WoodstockArts
10 9 8 7 6 5 4 3 2

WOODSTOCKARTS
P.O. Box 1342
Woodstock, NY 12498
T: 845-679-8111
F: 419-793-3452
Info@WoodstockArts.com
www.WoodstockArts.com
Telephone orders: 800-431-1579

CATALOGING IN PUBLICATION DATA
Roots of the 1969 Woodstock Festival : the backstory to "Woodstock"
/ edited by Weston Blelock, Julia Blelock ; foreword by Bob Fass.
160 p. : ill. ; 21 cm.
1. Woodstock Festival 2. Woodstock (NY) - History
I. Title. II. Blelock, Weston, 1949- III. Blelock, Julia, 1953-

ML38.W66 R66
                784.5
LCCN: 2009925109

Book design by ABIGAIL STURGES

ISBN 13: 978-0-9679268-5-8
ISBN 10: 0-9679268-5-8

Printed in the United States of America

Dedicated to people everywhere
who believe in the Woodstock State
of Mind—peace, love, music and art

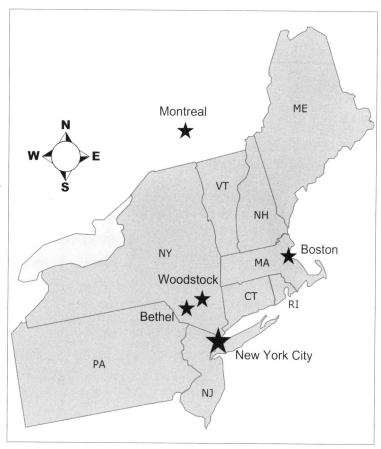

The northeastern United States. The town of **Woodstock** is about seventy miles from the 1969 festival site in **Bethel**, New York. Woodstock is one hundred miles from New York City and approximately two hundred and eighty miles from Montreal. © 2009 WoodstockArts.

Contents

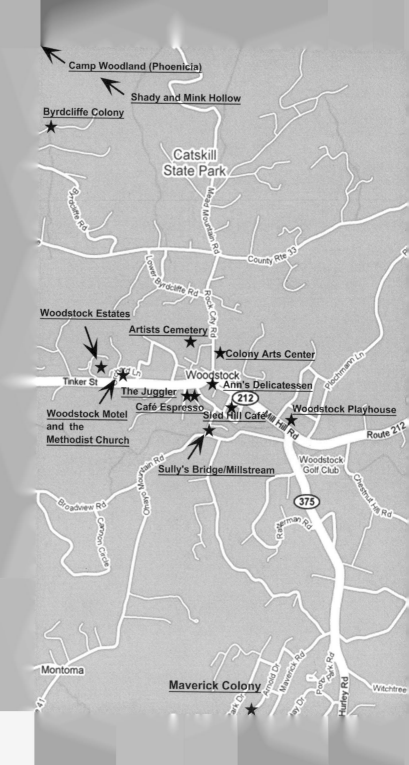

Camp Woodland (Phoenicia)

Shady and Mink Hollow

Byrdcliffe Colony

Catskill State Park

Byrdcliffe Rd

Mead Mountain Rd

County Rte 33

Lower Byrdcliffe Rd

Rock City Rd

Woodstock Estates

Artists Cemetery

Colony Arts Center

Plochmann Ln

Tinker St

Woodstock

Sled Ln

Ann's Delicatessen

212

The Juggler

Café Espresso

Sled Hill Café

Mill Hill Rd

Woodstock Playhouse

Route 212

Woodstock Motel
and the
Methodist Church

Sully's Bridge/Millstream

Woodstock
Golf Club

Chestnut Hill Rd

Ohayo Mountain Rd

375

Broadview Rd

Cannon Circle

Rauerman Rd

Montoma

Maverick Colony

Arnold Dr

Maverick Rd

Pond Park Rd

Hurley Rd

Witchtree

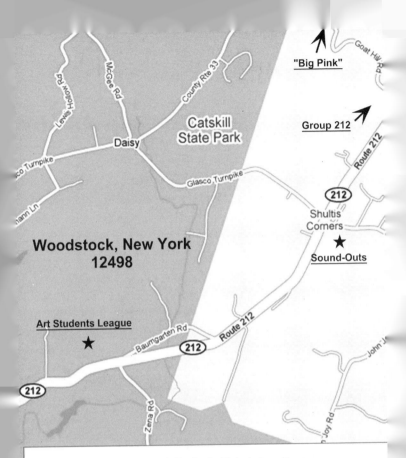

"Big Pink"

Group 212

Catskill
State Park

Route 212

212

Daisy

Glasco Turnpike

Shultis
Corners

★

Sound-Outs

Goat Hill Rd

McGee Rd

County Rte 33

Lewis Hollow Rd

Glasco Turnpike

Woodstock, New York
12498

Art Students League

★

Baumgarten Rd

Route 212

212

212

Zena Rd

John J

John Joy Rd

Roots of the 1969 Woodstock Festival—Historic Locations

Ann's Delicatessen, 1 Tinker Street (now the Corner Cupboard)
Art Students League, 2470 Route 212 (now the Woodstock School of Art)
Café Espresso, 59 Tinker Street (now the Center for Photography
 at Woodstock)
Colony Arts Center, 22 Rock City Road (now the Colony Café)
The Juggler, 65 Tinker Street (now Sole Mates Shoes)
Methodist Church, 132 Tinker Street (now the Tinker Street Cinema)
Woodstock Estates (now the Woodstock Post Office/Woodstock Meadows)
Woodstock Motel, 138 Tinker Street (no longer a motel)
Woodstock Playhouse, 103 Mill Hill Road

Foreword

Bob Fass

Before the 1969 Woodstock Festival there were the Sound-Outs.

They were to be a party, a happening. Something was happening, and some of us thought we knew what it was. Some of us had no idea it was happening. It was like what Dylan said about the UFO at the Sound-Out, or was it about the sixties? "Everyone was there but not everyone saw it." It was time for it to happen. The blues guitar and the honky-tonk piano met the electron. And with the light shows and the confluence of various liberating potions, there was the feeling that a new cultural mix was taking place. Along with this, there was the beautiful Woodstock valley and the town's history as a refuge and watershed and woodshed for artists and transgressors. The Chicago police rioters and the anti-warriors, the backpackers, the geniuses of the avant-garde, the 212'ers, the Rosebud Nation, Steam Punks and multimedia macrobiotic artists all came to the party in Pan Copeland's field. She danced to the pipes of Pan and all came to the party called Sound-Out. Someone from USCO called it Sound-Out because it wasn't a Be-In.

Late summer 1968. After signing *Radio Unnameable* off the air early on Saturday mornings, I'd pack my car full of hippie freak refugees from hot-time summer in the city and head up the thruway to Woodstock. The Town of Woodstock thought that there were altogether too many hippie freaks there already, gawking at musicians, so they said, "No sleeping in the fields and no concerts in the town limits."

Pan Copeland owned the delicatessen in the center of Woodstock and she cashed everybody's checks. She volunteered her farmhouse and land in Saugerties as a place for the festivities. Cat Mother and the All Night Newsboys, a band from the Lower East Side, came and took over Pan's farmhouse. We invited the

Friends of **Bob Fass** inscribed this graphically altered image of the emcee on the occasion of his first Sound-Out, "This is you at the Sound-Out (Saugerties Love-In) First Night, Happy Woodstock. Tom and Joanna Dawes." Courtesy of Bob Fass.

best musicians we knew. Stagehands built a stage. Macrobiotic, energy-transforming food was prepared and sold for pennies a bowl. Mind-expanding goulash imported from around the world was abundant. It was a potent mix of the new and the traditional. There was a whole lot of love and a whole lot of creativity and community spirit. As local performers' names were announced, international musicians wanted to appear and be part of this magic moment. Some stayed and became permanent residents of the area.

These weekends continued into the fall, until the weather made it impossible. I have a vague recollection that after the Nixonian Winter something similar happened the next year, only better. No one paid any admission. There were no souvenir programs. No T-shirts. No original-cast recordings. No movie except in our own minds, but a lot of people said they saw the UFO.

New York City, March 2009

Introduction

Weston Blelock

The Roots project began in March 2008 as an idea for the 2009 edition of the Woodstock Chamber of Commerce and Arts travel guide. Larry Lawrence, chair of the travel guide, had begun to solicit ideas for commemorating the fortieth anniversary of the 1969 festival. It occurred to me that a discussion by a panel of townspeople knowledgeable about events in the late sixties might be an interesting way to bring that era into focus and create some sound bites for the travel guide. In due course the Historical Society of Woodstock and the Chamber agreed to co-sponsor the panel discussion. I invited as panelists Michael Lang, the legendary promoter of the 1969 festival; Jean Young, co-author with Michael of *Woodstock Festival Remembered*; Bill West, a town official in the sixties; Jeremy Wilber, a bartender at the Sled Hill Café, a key rock 'n' roll watering hole in the sixties; and Paul McMahon, a musician and bona fide hippie. Geddy Sveikauskas, publisher of the *Woodstock Times*, agreed to serve as moderator. I developed a list of questions and vetted them with the six participants. The panel discussion was scheduled for August 9, 2008.

The event also included a musical component organized by Paul McMahon and me, featuring eighteen musical acts. As a result of the great turnout and the enthusiastic reception by the audience, I decided to publish the transcript of the panel discussion. It became clear that a photographic account of the players and events leading up to the 1969 festival would help to provide context for a number of themes and personalities touched upon during the discussion. The themes included Woodstock's glass-manufacturing era (early Arts and Crafts), the town's early musi-

Weston Blelock (upper right) at the Roots of '69 Woodstock Festival event held at the Colony Café, August 9, 2008. Moderator **Geddy Sveikauskas** is at upper left. Photo by Julia Blelock.

cal programs, the Byrdcliffe and Maverick art colonies, and the Sound-Outs.

Part of the profits of this book will be donated to the Historical Society of Woodstock and the Woodstock Chamber of Commerce and Arts, the sponsors of the panel discussion and contemporary Sound-Out.

Woodstock, March 2009

The Players

People and Groups Mentioned in the Panel Discussic

Happy and Artie Traum in concert. This photo appeared in the *Woodstock Week*, November 22, 1967. The duo was signed by Albert Grossman to his management company in 1970. Soon after, the brothers released their first album, *Happy and Artie Traum*. Photo courtesy of *Woodstock Week*.

Isaac Abrams Founder of the Coda Gallery in New York City, the world's first psychedelic art gallery.

Paul Albums Bass player for the rock band Fear Itself.

Swami Aumashananda Spiritual percussionist.

The Ballantines (Ian and Betty) Publishers/owners of Ballantine Books.

The Band Rock group that acted as back-up for Bob Dylan and is known for recordings such as *Music from Big Pink* and *The Band*.

Will Barnet Prolific American painter and graphic artist as well as an art teacher.

Ludwig Baumgarten Woodstock police constable in 1972.

The Beatles The Fab Four: George Harrison, John Lennon, Paul McCartney and Ringo Starr.

The Beats (the Beat Generation, Beatniks) American cultural non-conformists such as Jack Kerouac and Allen Ginsberg.

Karl Berger Vibist/pianist and co-founder of the Creative Music Studio.

The Blues Magoos New York's first psychedelic band.

Julius Bruggeman Sound-Out site manager and talent booker for 1968.

[Paul] Butterfield Electrifying blues harp player and leader of the Paul Butterfield Blues Band.

Children of God Chambers Brothers-like group active in the late sixties.

Pan Copeland Owner of Ann's Delicatessen, the Copeland Gallery and the West Saugerties farm where the Sound-Outs took place.

Walter Cronkite Anchorman of the *CBS Evening News* from 1962 to 1981.

Rick Danko Bassist for The Band.

Ram Dass Spiritual leader; author of *Remember, Be Here Now.*

Franklin "Bud" Drake An artist and Pan Copeland's son.

Will and Ariel Durant Authors of the eleven-volume *The Story of Civilization.*

Bob Dylan Iconic folk and rock musician.

Harry Edinger Commissioner of Health for Ulster County.

Peggy Egan Wife of John Egan, Woodstock Town Attorney.

Electric Lady Recording studio established in Greenwich Village in 1970 by Jimi Hendrix.

Jon Elliott Son of Nancy Chase and the actor Steven Elliott; principal photographer for *Woodstock Handmade Houses.*

Michael Esposito Lead guitarist for the Blues Magoos.

Alf Evers Woodstock Town Historian; author of *The Catskills: From Wilderness to Woodstock* and *Woodstock: History of an American Town.*

Bob Fass Host of *Radio Unnameable* on WBAI in New York City.

F. Scott Fitzgerald American novelist and short story writer.

Michael Foreman Man in charge of the program guide for the 1969 Woodstock Festival.

Jackson Frank Folksinger and writer.

Jean Gaede Local historian; author of *Woodstock Gatherings: Apple Bites and Ashes (Pre-1994)*.

Allen Ginsberg Beat poet; author of "Howl" (1956).

Milton Glaser Graphic designer.

Emma Goldman Russian-American anarchist leader.

Stanley Goldstein Headhunter and campgrounds coordinator, 1969 Woodstock Festival.

Peter Goodrich Man in charge of concessions, 1969 Woodstock Festival.

Albert Grossman Manager of Bob Dylan, The Band, Janis Joplin and other artists.

Sally Grossman Albert Grossman's wife.

Group 212 An arts organization directed by John "Bob" Liikala.

Tim Hardin Folk musician and composer.

Rush Harp Woodstock man-about-town.

Jimi Hendrix Hard rock guitarist, singer and songwriter.

Milton Houst Woodstock Town Supervisor from 1968 to 1972.

Michael Jeffery Jimi Hendrix's manager.

Jerry Jerominek Local designer; operator of a sign company.

Fred Johnston Antiques dealer in Kingston, New York.

James Joyce Renowned Irish writer.

Kleinert Performance space associated with the Woodstock Guild; now known as the Kleinert/James Arts Center.

Elliott Landy Rock music photographer.

Timothy Leary Icon of sixties counterculture; LSD promoter.

Jack Lemmon Hollywood actor.

John Richard "Jackie" Lomax British guitarist, singer and songwriter.

Sara Lowndes Bob Dylan's wife.

Karl Marx Author of *The Communist Manifesto*.

Peter Max Multidimensional artist.

Vern May Woodstock Town Supervisor from 1972 to 1975.

Victor Maymudes Bob Dylan's road manager and traveling companion.

Ellen McIlwaine Singer/songwriter and musician; best known as a slide guitarist.

Gene Meyer Owner of the Corner Cupboard, a Woodstock deli known during the sixties as Ann's Delicatessen.

John "Jocko" Moffitt Co-founder of the Sound-Outs; event producer in 1967 and 1968 (March).

Fred Neil Blues and folk singer and songwriter.

Bobby Neuwirth Singer, songwriter and visual artist.

Marc Plate Son of Bud and Gladys Plate, local artists; is currently the town tax assessor.

Ramblin' Jack Elliott Folksinger.

Ken Reynolds Owner of Ken's Exxon, a local garage.

Susie Reynolds Daughter-in-law of Ken Reynolds.

Guru Rinpoche Known in India as Padmasambhava.

John Roberts A financial backer of the 1969 Woodstock Festival.

[Nelson] Rockefeller Governor of New York from 1959 to 1973.

Jay Rolison Candidate for New York State office.

Rolling Stones Famous British rock group.

Robert Roskind Author of *Memoirs of an Ex-Hippie: Seven Years in the Counterculture.*

Swami Satchidananda Indian religious figure; founder of the Integral Yoga movement.

John Sebastian Songwriter and harmonica player; a co-founder of the Lovin' Spoonful.

James T. Shotwell Historian and professor of international relations at Columbia University.

Paul Siebel Singer, songwriter and guitarist.

Bud Sife Owner and manager of the Sled Hill Café, one of Woodstock's principal music venues during the sixties.

Paul Simon Songwriter and musician.

Judson Smith Painter and teacher.

Alexander Tapooz Motel owner in Woodstock.

Roger Tillison Musician.

Artie Traum Folk musician: guitarist and songwriter. Brother of Happy Traum.

Happy (Harry Peter) Traum Folk musician: songwriter, guitarist and banjo player. Brother of Artie Traum.

Mark Twain Author of such classics as *The Adventures of Tom Sawyer* and *The Adventures of Huckleberry Finn.*

Elbert Varney Vice President of the National Bank of Orange and Ulster Counties, a local bank.

Gail Varsi A co-founder of Family of Woodstock; her telephone number became a hotline for visitors to the town following the 1969 festival.

Alan Watts British philosopher and comparative religion specialist.

Jim Young Co-owner of The Juggler, avant-garde purveyor of books, records, and art and music supplies.

Chris Zaloom Lead guitarist for Fear Itself.

Zane Zimmerman Manager and counterman at Carey's Deli in Woodstock.

The August 9, 2008, Panel Discussion

Roots of '69 panelists. From left: **Michael Lang**, **Jean Young**, **Bill West** and **Jeremy Wilber**. Moderator **Geddy Sveikauskas** is in right foreground. Photo by Dion Ogust.

Weston Blelock Good afternoon . . . I'm Weston Blelock and I'm with the Historical Society of Woodstock. The Roots of '69 Woodstock Festival program will begin with a backstory panel discussion, which will be followed immediately by a contemporary Sound-Out. Recently, *Rolling Stone* magazine rated the Woodstock Festival of 1969 as one of fifty historic moments in rock 'n' roll. Today we are going to hear from our all-star panel of Michael Lang, Jean Young, Bill West, Jeremy Wilber and Paul McMahon about the events leading up to the festival. Geddy Sveikauskas is our moderator. Won't you please help me welcome our distinguished panel and moderator?

Geddy Sveikauskas (GS) All right, distinguished panel. This is going to be a bit more of a scripted event than I had anticipated. But since considerable preparation, it is alleged, went into the preparation of the questions with you, I'll try to stick to that, at least for a start.

However, I did look at the last page—you always look at the bottom line. And there's a part that says, "All." And "All" consists of two questions. So, although I won't ask the panel these, I think they're good not only for the panel but for everyone here to think about.

And "All" question one is, How did the 1969 festival influence your thinking—did it make you hopeful or depressed? And question two is, How does that era manifest itself in your life today?

I think you're all living evidence of how it manifests itself in your life today, as are this group of hardy survivors up here.

Michael Lang is probably the best person to start off giving his stuff, because he was so important organizing this. At the time that I first saw Michael he was, I guess, what, eighteen or nineteen? He was pretty young. And he had this tremendous dynamism and energy that impressed everybody. But we didn't think that he could pull off what he did, of course. And what he did, I guess, did as much to change our lives as his.

So here we go, Michael. Here are the questions that were prepared with you.

Roots of (69) WOODSTOCK FESTIVAL

August 9, 2008

Backstory Panel Discussion and Soundout

Colony Café
22 Rock City Road, Woodstock, NY

12:30 to 2:30 p.m.

Moderator:
Geddy Sveikauskas
Publisher, *Woodstock Times* and other newspapers

Panel:

Michael Lang
Woodstock resident and legendary '69 Festival promoter

Jean Young
co-author with Lang of *Woodstock Festival Remembered*

Bill West
who was in local government in the 1960s

Jeremy Wilber
former Town Supervisor, who was tending bar during the late sixties at the Sled Hill Café

Paul McMahon
iconic local musician and Mothership impresario

The subject of the discussion will be the events leading up to the Woodstock Festival of 1969, including the Soundout festivals that took place in and around Woodstock for several years in the late 1960s.

FREE EVENT

Contemporary Soundout
2:45 to 5:00 p.m.

Produced by
Paul McMahon

The following musical acts are scheduled to appear:

Hair of the Dog
Beki Brindle
Joey Eppard
Frankie and his Fingers
Spiv

Paul McMahon
Peter Walker
Jeremy Bernstein
 of Stoney Clove Lane
Ben Vita
Naked
and more

Sponsored by:
Historical Society of Woodstock and the Woodstock Chamber of Commerce & Arts

WOODSTOCK NY
Chamber of
Commerce & Arts
woodstockchamber.com

Historical Society of Woodstock
woodstockhistory.org

For more information call: 845.679.8111

Roots of '69 poster for the August 9, 2008, panel discussion and contemporary Sound-Out. Poster designed by Naomi Schmidt of www.naomigraphics.com. Courtesy of WoodstockArts Archives.

Panelist **Michael Lang** on August 9, 2008. Photo by Dion Ogust.

After the success of the Miami Pop Festival, what drew you to Woodstock?

Michael Lang (**ML**) I guess I was ready to move on from Florida. I lived there for three years. I was from New York. I liked New York, and I wanted to be close to New York, but not really right in it. And Woodstock was very similar to the town of Coconut Grove [Miami] in Florida. It was an artists' community. It was a small, kind of lazy community. I had been to Woodstock as a child when my parents used to come through Woodstock to see the galleries and when we would take trips to Canada, so I kind of knew it.

There was a very vital music scene going on here, so I was just drawn to come here.

GS Alf Evers, the great Woodstock historian, said [that] as far as he knew Woodstock was the only small community in the world that had two worldwide famous cultural things happening, and that was the artists in the twenties, for the most part, and the Maverick festivals then, and then the music scene in the sixties and seventies. And Alf always claimed that if it happened some place twice it could happen a third time, only we don't know its manifestation yet.

And I think we kind of know we have that in mind. Ecstatic moments come not too frequently, and they come sometimes surprisingly and spontaneously, and that's the wonderful thing about them, and, you know, they really affect our lives.

So the Woodstock you found was the Woodstock I found—that is, a community of maybe three thousand souls with some older artists, for the most part, and some younger musicians. And people who came to watch, to see the older artists and the younger musicians. And then there were the IBMers. And then there were the natives. Right? As I remember it.

ML That's right. That's exactly right.

GS And it's the mix that makes Woodstock so wonderful. It's not just the artists, it's everybody. How did the festivals like the Maverick and the Sound-Outs inspire and guide your thinking?

ML Well, I think greatly. The Sound-Outs were kind of the spark for the Woodstock festival in that it got me thinking about doing the concerts here. I'd done a series of concerts in Florida and then the festival. The Sound-Outs just had a great feel, and it was in the

Poster for a picnic at
Pan Copeland's farm.
Courtesy of Ruth Drake.

country and it provided all the guidelines that I needed. I was sort of thinking of a broader event but with the same kind of emotional impact. So it had a lot to do with our early thinking.

GS And how about the Maverick festivals? Did you know anything about them at the time?

ML I did. Jean and Jim [Young] sort of educated me to a lot of that history . . . The reason it became a music and art fair, frankly, was because of the background of this town and the Maverick festivals.

Three chums at a **Maverick festival** gathering circa 1920.
Photo courtesy of Woodstock Library.

Panelists **Michael Lang, Jean Young** and **Jeremy Wilber**. Photo by Dion Ogust.

GS The Sound-Outs, as you may know, were located near the Peter Pan Farm and other places like that. The only thing Michael did—and it was a modest change—was to increase the audience by about a thousand times. And that had certain consequences of its own, as we all know, right?

Who's Peter Goodrich—I remember Peter Goodrich—and what impact did he have?

ML Peter was a friend of mine from Coconut Grove. A lot of people from the Grove came up when we started to work on the show. And he was an antiques dealer. He was a kind of . . . I don't know how you'd describe Peter.

Jean Young (JY) World-wise.

ML Yeah, world-wise. And his contribution to the festival was just being a quick thinker and someone I could trust. He helped organize some of the art exhibits. He helped organize the concessions, which started out being wares and ended up being other kinds of

Audience for the **Roots of '69** panel discussion held August 9, 2008, at the Colony Café. Photo by Julia Blelock.

wares. And he was just someone that I could depend upon to help me through most of the insanity.

GS So you had cultural contacts, obviously, in the music community. And you also had friends, people like Jim and Jean, who formed an important bridge to the community at that time. How did you get in contact with Jim and what was that relationship like?

ML I met them at The Juggler. They had a great shop in town with music and books. We just met in the shop and became friends, and I started telling them about my ideas and I asked Jim to help me out. We started to look for a location, because he seemed to have a good knowledge of the area and liked to poke around, like

I did, on back roads. And we spent several months looking for potential sites and we never actually found one in Woodstock.

The Woodstock festival was called "Woodstock" for several reasons. One: we intended to be here. And two: the name sort of embodied a lot of the feelings and imagery that we wanted to conjure in promoting this festival. It said the right things about what we were trying to do, and so although we never found a site I decided to keep the name, because it was important to us.

GS   It's ironic, isn't it? People have never gotten over that. Woodstock and Bethel, Bethel and Woodstock.

How about the musicians? Who did you know? Did you know Albert [Grossman] at that time?

ML   I met Albert, because, you know, I moved to Woodstock in the early spring of '68, and I met Albert, and I met Tim Hardin—through Jim and Jean—and Rick Danko and a bunch of the guys from The Band. It was a small, very sort of laid-back scene in those days. People weren't hiding out yet. So it was easy to connect and it felt great to be part of the community. And all of that supported my confidence in going ahead with this.

GS   It must have been quite an experience to know that not only was the community changed after a while when people would come and gawk, but that you had a big part in changing it. It's ironic, isn't it?

ML   Yes, it is.

GS   Tell me about the recording studio stuff. I know that in Woodstock, at that time, there . . . got to be several recording studios over time, and they became part of the business and part of the life . . . Imagine living in the country and having your recording studio right there. That's pretty interesting.

ML   I don't think there were any real studios at that time. The studios were mostly located in big cities, because it was a commercials business. Music was a part of it, but their bread and butter were commercials—radio and television. And I sort of felt that . . . especially in Woodstock, because there were so many musicians living here and attracted to the town . . . that there was a need for it. People wanted to get away from the urban atmosphere and create in a more laid-back setting, and so I thought, let's build a studio.

GS I know I liked Woodstock immediately because I saw so many faces I knew from the West Village and later from the East Village. You know, "This can't be so bad for the countryside." It was just beautiful. It was so kind of idyllic but somehow so familiar as well. Electric Lady. There were musicians [in] both places, and so people like me felt comfortable. And of course there was the wider cultural movement at that time, so it was not just music but a whole thing.

Here's one I don't know the answer to: who was Alexander Tapooz?

ML Alexander Tapooz was an Armenian rug dealer who owned the property that I bought to build the studio.

Before that, I think it was called Tapooz Country Inn, and for a number of years I think it was a dance studio. They used to have dances there, in this big open studio building. And eventually he came to store his rugs. When I bought it, it was kind of defunct but still a great space.

GS I've got to read this one word-for-word, because it's like a term paper. This is the last question for you, Michael. You've been great answering them.

"There's been much speculation about how the name of the festival was chosen. Supposedly Michael Foreman and Stanley Goldstein said the name had to 'convey a sense of freedom, both of thought and physical presence.' And you were to have replied, 'We gotta keep the name Woodstock. It really has a mystical feeling about it'." Please comment, in five hundred words or less.

James T. Shotwell memorial in the Woodstock Artists Cemetery. Photo by Julia Blelock.

Inscription on the James T. Shotwell memorial. Photo by Julia Blelock.

ML Well, I think I was always committed to calling it "Woodstock." From its conception it was conceived to be here for a reason, and that reason was what the town was about and what I hoped the festival would bring to its attendees and what they could expect when they got here. So it was never going to be anything but Woodstock. I fought a lot of battles with a lot of people along the way, who wanted to change the name, first to Wallkill and then to Bethel, but it was always going to be Woodstock.

GS I hope you all have visited the Woodstock Artists Cemetery across the street more than once, because most of the members of the arts community are planted there and the legend at the top of it, written by a Roosevelt brain-truster, is the famous "They lie here encircled by the everlasting hills who contributed through this, that and the other thing, and really through their lives, to this area and to America." It's a truly wonderful little memorial without being a memorial at all.

Okay, Bill West. Even at that time, at a young age, you were the former Town Supervisor of Woodstock, is that not right?

Bill West (BW) Correct.

GS Having gotten the job at the age of twelve . . . and this was before the years of Mr. Houst and of Vern May, so you are really part of the old Woodstock political and social establishment . . . so this must have been quite an addition to your life as well.

BW Well, it got our attention, Geddy. We were quite familiar with what Pan Copeland had on the intersection of 212 and Glasco Turnpike. She'd been running these music events for a period of time. And I think most of us who were involved in local government had visited that facility and that activity over the time. We were really not concerned about it, because I don't think I ever saw more than maybe a couple of hundred people there . . .

GS It seemed harmless, and most of all it was in Saugerties!

BW Yes! And when we heard about Michael Lang's venture at what we called the Tapooz Country Club, we assumed it was going to be something very similar, with a couple of hundred people, so we were not overly concerned. And eventually we started hearing reports out of New York City that there were going to be five thousand, ten thousand, fifteen thousand, fifty thousand people. My God! What are we going to do? So everybody got pretty haired up. And I think the County Health people talked to Michael about it and pretty much determined that there was no appropriate place in Woodstock for it to be . . . once the venue was moved we were

Panelists **Michael Lang**, **Bill West**, **Jeremy Wilber** and **Paul McMahon**.
Photo by Dion Ogust.

truly concerned about the name Woodstock, because that would
be on everybody's note—"We're going to go to Woodstock," not
Bethel. I mean, "We're going to head to Woodstock." So we talked
about various means of keeping people out of Woodstock and
directing them to Bethel, and I think we talked about having signs
up and doing some advertising, et cetera, et cetera. But truly concerned about five, ten, fifteen thousand people coming to our
community, when the music festival at that time was either going
to be, I think, initially in Wallkill, and then they moved over to
Bethel. But it was of deep concern to us, Geddy. And I think . . .
if we thought fifty thousand people were going to come in to
Woodstock today, we'd all dive into the shelters.

GS So here's this wonderful, beautiful symbol of freedom and
expression called Woodstock and there are signs all over it:
"Woodstock That Way," "Woodstock Somewhere Else."

TOURISTS! YOU STILL HERE?

10¢   **JULY 31**
                                                                  1954

THE ONLY PAPER IN WOODSTOCK THAT ISN'T AFRAID

The Wasp was published by Holly Cantine and Dachine Rainer. A sequence of headlines began on July 10, 1954, with "Tourists, Go Home!" It continued on July 31 with "Tourists! You Still Here?" and ended on August 21 with "You Have Been Warned." Courtesy of Woodstock Library.

BW Well, you know, Geddy, there was a paper called *The Wasp* in Woodstock, and one of the headlines was, "Tourists Go Home," if you recall that one.

GS Yup, that was even before Jeremy's time.

Jeremy Wilber (JW) Jeremy remembers *The Wasp*.

GS I think the artistic community was in kind of a strange place, because I think a lot of the ones who had been around didn't want the town disturbed. However, they did like the vision of freedom that Michael and his cohorts represented.

BW There was some history to having unusual activities in Woodstock. If you go back, before the war, to the old Maverick festivals that were quite unique, kind of a quasi-Mardi Gras . . .

In the community, people dressed up in costumes and wandered around. And it was a multi-day festival, which I don't [personally] recall but people have told me about it. So that history was there for activities of a unique nature.

GS What did people at the Country Club and at the County Board of Supervisors at that time think about the whole thing? What was their attitude? Did they know much about it?

BW Well, as I mentioned, Geddy, we in the community here, we were pretty much aware of what Pan Copeland was doing, and we thought Michael's Woodstock festival was going to be just a manifestation of that—maybe on a little grander scale; maybe he'd have five hundred people, you know . . . And then we started getting reports back from people reading the papers—the *New York Times*, et cetera, et cetera—that this was going to be a much grander event, and then it got up to ten, fifteen, twenty, fifty thousand people. At that point we were truly concerned about it. And my recollection is that Milton [Houst] and the County Health people had a meeting with you to find out what was going on. Is that your recollection?

ML Yeah. As I said, we never found a location that worked. So they were very happy to hear that.

BW Well, we were still concerned, Michael . . . Actually, I'll tell you a funny story. Not too many years ago I was driving down Mead's Mountain Road and it was raining. There was a car from North Carolina in front of me with a big sign in the back window saying, "Just Married." And they were obviously lost so I pulled up in front of them and said, "May I help you?" And the young couple said, "Yeah, where was the festival?" On their honeymoon they were looking for the Woodstock festival. So, many, many years afterwards the people in the world were still looking for Woodstock and thinking they were going to see some magical thing here . . . and they might have.

GS "Where was the festival?" That would be the question. They'd usually roll down the window and say, "Where was the festival?"

BW You still get it today.

GS Let's do a mention of the hippie problem. There was not only the musical scene, but there were these people in their twenties whose social mores were a little bit different [from those of] most of the local people. And, what's more, there was another problem. They didn't have any money. It was a real problem. That's not the kind of tourist Woodstock was exactly looking for. And it turned out, of course, that, by the kind of revenge that history brings about, a lot of these people became shopkeepers in Woodstock and then they formed the Woodstock Independent Party and then they took over the Democratic Party and then they defeated the Republicans eventually.

BW So *that's* what happened!

GS That must have been an unwelcome change in your life, Bill.

BW We shall return. [laughter]

GS That's right. The tide will go the other way.

BW I think that was one of the obvious things that you could see as a result of the Woodstock festival. There were cute little boutiques and stores in the late sixties. And after the Woodstock festival I think we saw a fair number of head shops, hippies sleeping on the Village Green and on people's lawns. It became somewhat of a problem for a few years, and luckily it changed dramatically and I think we have some real fine shopkeepers in the community now. But there was a period of time in '70, maybe '71 or '72, in that particular era, when it was of deep concern, I think.

GS At one time I think Peggy Egan had a meeting. Did you attend that, or what did you think of it?

BW No, I didn't, but I was aware of it.

ML You know, what was interesting was that it didn't happen in Bethel. You'd have expected that to be the place for people to come in and look for it to happen.

GS Well, we in Woodstock were early discoverers of the NIMBY [not in my back yard] thing . . . that this stuff was great as long as it wasn't here. So in a certain sense Bethel provided a wonderful thing. It had the Woodstock name but that was it, and we could be snooty about how people would ask us where the festival was and stuff like that, but it hadn't really affected us. It's almost as though we had arranged for it to take place so that it wouldn't affect the beauty and tranquility of our community, real or alleged.

BW You know, I think Woodstock—the name—for some reason or other has a certain cachet as opposed to Bethel. Bethel doesn't have a very great ring to it, does it? Well, Woodstock has been an artists' colony from the days of Hervey White and the Maverick . . . before Byrdcliffe . . . for how many years, Geddy? Since the early 1900s, right? 1800s? Before my time.

GS Alf's claim was that the original Bohemians were literally the Bohemian glass-makers. The people who made the glass had these glass factories in Shady, and they would keep the production going all night, because you had to, to make what they made, and then all the farm kids would come from all over the land to stay up all night and watch the glass-blowers. According to Alf [Evers], those were the first Bohemians.

BW Well, we as young kids could go to the stream . . . and we swam in Shady, and you could pick up shards of glass that had come down from the glassworks, and we used to throw them at

Shards of aquamarine glass from the old Shady glass factories.
Courtesy of WoodstockArts Archives.

each other as young people. Now I'd love to have a couple of them sitting on my mantel, but they're not to be found.

GS Shady Blue, right? I think maybe [Fred] Johnston had some of this in Kingston.

BW Oh, did he?

GS He had a few pieces, allegedly, yeah.
   You were a County Health Inspector?

BW No.

GS It says here, "As a County Health Inspector, were you called up to Tapooz's?" Can you recall what transpired after that? Denies all knowledge, right?

BW I'm sorry?

GS Denies all knowledge of that? Do you recall?

BW Well, we spoke to the Health people. Harry Edinger was the Commissioner of Health at that time, and I think he may have spoken to Michael Lang, because, again, you know, we were thinking fifty thousand people, which was beyond our comprehension in town here.

GS A lot of Porta Toilets, right? Well, the closest we got, of course, was when they had the revival at Saugerties.

BW Yes.

GS There were enough people that it wasn't just an echo of the original festival . . . we had a chance to see what it was like to have it real close.

ML We estimated that it was close to three hundred and seventy thousand. We had several meetings with the Town then as well, thinking that people were going to be pouring in to Woodstock. I kept saying, "Kids go where the music is." I don't think there was much of an impact from that weekend.

BW Although they did shut off the road a little bit, directing them . . .

ML There was an extensive traffic plan—that we paid for, actually—circling people around the center of town. It just never got used. And the legend of the traffic jams . . . closing the Thruway and the Canadian borders . . . followed us around quite a bit. And so they wouldn't let us park anybody near the site in Saugerties. We were parking people up to two hours away. There were two thousand buses, shuttles. It was absurd.

Official **New York State Highways** sign seen on a barn near the southbound exit of the New York Thruway at Route 32. Photo by Julia Blelock.

GS Yup.

ML And there wasn't a car on the streets the whole weekend.

GS That's right.

BW Talking about traffic jams . . . my son came in from college [in August '69]. He and three or four friends went over and they parked within five miles of Bethel and walked in and stayed the first day. And they came back to where their car was and they couldn't get it out—couldn't go back down [Route] 17 or anything. And so he called me up, and we had done some work, built some bridges in Claryville and over in that area, so I knew the back roads, and we went over to Peekamoose and picked them up in Grahamsville, I believe, and brought them out that way, because they couldn't have gotten out any other way.

GS The big Woodstock weekend, [and] Woodstock was very quiet.

Now, as you all know, there are a variety of communities that have associations with Woodstock, with the kind of people that come to Woodstock—you know, Big Sur, Taos, Key West, I guess Coconut Grove, Michael, right? And Provincetown, Berkeley. Jean, you are alleged to have arrived in Woodstock in 1963 from

Berkeley via Provincetown and New York City. Can you compare what you found in Woodstock vis-à-vis the California scene?

JY Well, we came from California earlier, and we lived in New York [City] for three years.

GS Ah, in the Village?

JY It was really for the art scene . . . We had a child, and a lot of people my age that had children like me wanted to move out of New York. They didn't want to stay. And so some of them moved to Provincetown, and we came to Woodstock because it was an artists' community. It was known as one of the only ones on the east coast. So we came here, and there were still artists . . . certainly the ones that were almost famous came—from the twenties and thirties—but there were still people from the forties and fifties who had reputations here. And for us it was an artists' community. But once we got here we realized that the musicians that came here were more advanced in what they were doing. They were doing more creative things than the artists were doing. So it shifted for us, to things more concentrated on music as the creative force of Woodstock shifted. Actually, music has become more important than art here. It was established as an art community but then had the music as well, which was really great.

And then of course the hippies came in . . . new thinking, anti-war sentiment . . . and then of course Michael along with it. And I must say, when he came in to town and we were in our bookstore and he was looking for some place to rent for land . . . none of the real estate people in town really took him seriously. Like, he didn't have any money. He wasn't properly this or that. And so we thought, we'll help him out, and my husband went around, as Michael said, looking for a place for a festival. And it just kept getting bigger, the idea became bigger and bigger, and that's why, as Mike has said, that's why it moved out, because there was no place for it here. But the cultural center of his festival was based in Woodstock. It wasn't a Bethel place. It was because of the whole community here. It was because of the whole community, and what had come in to this place.

ML We were not the Bethel Generation.

JY And so people say, well, why Woodstock? Well, because spiritually, and I hate to use that word, but this is where it was. This is where the things took place . . . back to the land. So people wanted to get away from New York [and] back to the land was part of it. It just all jelled together. It wasn't one thing or another. It was everything that happened. Well, fortunately, we were right in the middle of it, being on the street.

GS It was clearly a generational time, you know. This was before Family of Woodstock. Woodstock still had a constabulary rather than a police force. And I remember coming in to town and meeting a little old lady, whose name I never found out. She looked up at me and said, "You people think you've invented it all, don't you? Well, if you had lived here thirty years ago you'd have seen what an arts town really was like." And she was referring to the Maverick, of course. And the Maverick, in the tradition of kind of looseness and expression, was really important in Woodstock. There's a picture somewhere of a masted boat that had been built by everybody. They had spent all summer building the scenery for the festival. I think . . . Jean [Gaede]—it was maybe 1924, I'm not sure—but as I heard it there was one performance and as a part of the performance they burnt the ship that they had spent all summer building.

Jean Gaede (from the audience) *The Pirate Ship.* They built the boat and at the end they set it on fire and destroyed it.

GS So imagine that . . . spending all summer doing something and then burning it down. That's very Woodstock.

ML Roots of Burning Man.

The *Ark Royale* under construction for a production of Walter Steinhilber's **The Pirate Ship** in 1924. The eighty-foot-long by sixty-foot-tall vessel was built over the summer and burned during the single performance. Postcard courtesy of Historical Society of Woodstock.

GS At The Juggler, I remember that round sign. What kind of business was that for you? Was it like a kind of entrée to the town?

JY It was a learning experience, because we had opened it . . . what do we want to put in the store? Books . . . and art supplies. It was a learning experience, because the people who came to town would tell us what they were reading. We were more or less after the Beat Generation, so we were part of the leftovers of that. We were between the Beats and the hippies.

GS Right. The Beatles, they called them.

JY So we had an inkling of this migration from the Beat to the hippie movement, and we had the books for these people. We were the first people to have *Rolling Stone* up here, and the *Whole Earth Catalog*, and then when the music people kept wanting music we started ordering the records that people wanted, and so that included the Beatles and so that is how far that went.

GS Did you sell copies of *On the Road*?

JY Well, certainly. But I must say, some of the things that we thought would sell and that people would want to read—some of the old classics—basically they wanted other books. Whatever they wanted, then, this is what we would have. So we kind of grew with the town and grew with what they wanted, and when the musicians needed strings for their guitars, we ordered the strings. We kind of kept up with what was happening. We were providing what people wanted—and a lot of what they wanted were things we wanted.

GS What about books about Buddhism and Tibetans?

JY There was Alan Watts. I studied with Alan Watts in San Francisco. There was that early part, but not much. It was the musicians, who were basically interested in poetry and in the records. And of course yoga was good and psychology was good. I remember you coming from Harvard. Did you come from Harvard?

GS Shhh, let's not get into that. Timothy Leary and I spent some time in Millbrook.

JY Okay.

GS Yes, there was clearly a connection between social ideas and this sense of travel and of learning about yourself by learning about the country, from Mark Twain to Fitzgerald to the Beats to Allen Ginsberg . . . and it was just a part of America, and it still is.

Elliott Landy (from the audience) I came here in '68 to photograph Bob Dylan and The Band and a lot of the other musicians . . . But what I want to say is [that] when I got here, to Woodstock, it was full of macrobiotic restaurants and health food stores, even more so than music.

Jim Young behind the counter at The Juggler. Photo appeared in the *Woodstock Week* of December 7, 1967.

It was originally founded as a utopian society in 1903, and the beauty of the festival was that this utopian community was not limited to music—music was part of it, as it had a lot of great music concerts over the years—but the reason why Woodstock was honored was because of the appropriate nature of what the town was about; at least that was my experience at the time.

GS Okay. Let me get back to the questioning, okay? I'm sorry to do this to you, Elliott, but that's true—I think everybody had their own Woodstock, everybody has their own agenda, and at the time of so much change there were plenty of followers for lots of different ideas.

Now, Jean, did you go to the Sound-Outs or to Group 212 activities? Please tell us a little bit about that.

JY Well, it was just nice to go and lie down on a blanket and take your blanket and your friends and listen to the music. It was very relaxed and informal and it was a great thing to do. And the people that were playing there were all people we wanted to hear and it was great.

Stage and audience at the first **Sound-Out**, Labor Day 1967.
Photo appeared in the *Woodstock Week* of September 7, 1967.

ML Who did you see there?

JY I think we saw Tim [Hardin], I think the Blues Magoos. I can't remember. Really, we weren't so much into . . . being specific about it. It was just such a great outing, to be able to go out and hear music.

GS Did you and Michael ever go out to any Sound-Outs and experience it together?

JY No, I don't think so.

ML I went with Jim once.

JY Did you?

BW Was that Pan's facility?

Sound-Out audience on Labor Day 1967. Photo appeared in the *Woodstock Week* of September 7, 1967.

ML Yeah.

GS In 1979 you and Michael co-wrote a book entitled *Woodstock Festival Remembered*. Do you recall if Michael mentioned how the early Woodstock festivals might have influenced his thinking?

JY Well, that's kind of obvious, that it would have. I mean . . . it was in the air, and it was here and it would have to have been part of anybody's thinking. Not specifically or scientifically on paper, but because, certainly, it was here. His story is the story of coming from Florida and coming up here.

GS I haven't thought for many years of the name Bud Sife of Sled Hill Café.

JY Wow! Yeah!

GS Jeremy . . . growing up in Woodstock . . . what was the impact of the musicians on your life and on your experiences?

JW Well, before answering that let me just say, with respect to the preparations for this event. A fine response . . . with the opening ceremonies for the Olympics in Beijing [also taking place on August 9]. Congratulations. This is wonderful.

Since you asked the question. [shows Sled Hill Café posters]

GS Ha ha, terrific. There's Quasha . . . Children of God.

JW These posters, by the way, were done by the Woodstock postermaker Jerry Jerominek. You'll notice this font. The only place in Woodstock you'll see a vestige of this is on the building of the Woodstock Cinema . . . that's a Jerry Jerominek font that was carried over from when that cinema was an art cinema located in what is now the Kleinert.

GS What year do you think that was?

JW This poster is either '69 or '70. Ellen McIlwaine, I'm sure, played at the Sound-Outs. She was in a group then called Fear Itself.

GS Yup.

JW Paul Albums was the bass player in that group, God rest him.

PM Chris Zaloom.

JW Yeah, Chris Zaloom. You know, before answering your question specifically, because I see a couple of my peers—Marc Plate and Jon Elliott and maybe some others that I just don't spot from here—I just want to say the experience *I* had when I was nineteen years old, when the Woodstock festival happened . . . I didn't go . . . I was here in Woodstock for the Woodstock festival . . .

Panelist **Jeremy Wilber** with his Sled Hill Café poster and sign.
Photo by Dion Ogust.

Because memory is so unreliable I put on my forty-year-old hat and I wore the costume of the time to try and jar it, and what *I* remember about that era, or what I *think* I remember about that era—somebody mentioned Millbrook—was that the youth in Woodstock . . . and Marc and Jon, you can correct me if I'm wrong here . . .

But growing up in Woodstock . . . the kids in Woodstock, although we didn't necessarily have a community of view we certainly had a consanguinity of mind, and this was because we went to the Onteora School and the Onteora School district was comprised of Woodstock and the towns of Olive, Shandaken and Hurley. Woodstock . . . because of its unique cultural history and also because it was right on the route of the New York City bus, on Route 212 . . . was daily provided with New York media, the New York City papers. Plus the art scene we had here . . . We were treated very, very, very differently in the school district from the kids in the other towns. We used to joke then that the people in Shandaken still ate out of wooden bowls and they skinned dogs, and at that time I don't think it was very far from being true.

Jeremy Wilber displays the Roots of '69 T-shirt design at the Woodstock Library Fair, July 27, 2008. Photo by Julia Blelock.

The experience of growing up in Woodstock was very, very unique. And again, you were treated very differently in the school district and this forced upon us a consanguinity that might otherwise not have prevailed.

My memory of Woodstock's coming to prominence and its culmination in the festival was not surprise, not even pride, it was sort of like, well, you know, okay, *finally*. We . . . grew up with such a feeling . . . I guess the best word to use to describe it is smugness. We just felt that we were very, very, very hip. I don't know if we were or not, but we felt that way. We felt very different and very informed. Woodstock, as I mentioned, had an art cinema then. While we were watching *The Seventh Seal* all the other kids in school were watching *Under the Yum Yum Tree* with Jack Lemmon, just to give you an idea of how culturally separate the kids in Woodstock were from all the other kids in the area . . .

So I don't remember any of us feeling surprised to see the town become a symbol of what it was.

GS Jeremy, as time went on people bought more second homes in places further out than Woodstock, right? Some in Shandaken and some in other places. It was a mix of native people and second-homers that was very nice. But then it somehow got unbalanced and there were more of the new people, some of whom still made their livings in the city. The people who moved out had known this land for a hundred and fifty years or so. What did that feel like?

JW Well, the second-home experience in Woodstock is not unique. I used to rake leaves back in the fifties for second-home owners—people who could afford my labors at twenty-five cents an hour. What a lot of people find hard to believe, [those] who didn't grow up here, is in the fifties into the early sixties—and, Bill, I'm sure you'll remember this—there was actually quite a bit of need in Woodstock. It wasn't the wealthy community that we think of it [as] now. What I remember most about one experience growing up in Woodstock . . . I was brought up by a single mom, and one of the houses we rented one winter was one of those fusty old shacks up in Byrdcliffe, and of course those buildings weren't originally built for winter habitation. Well, the cure for that, you see, was kerosene heaters about the size of a VW bus, and that's how you got through, or shivered through, a winter up there. There was a lot more coal, a lot more kerosene, and there was a lot more need in those days. And people who could afford a second home generally meant somebody who wanted a second bathroom, which meant that we were getting hired to install these things. We were very happy. My first job in Woodstock after I turned eighteen was tending bar in a restaurant, and we just would have died without these people coming. So my experience, and the experience of many of the people I grew up with, who made livings off of this demographic in fact, was not resistance . . . it wasn't "Oh gosh, things were better then"; it was, rather, welcoming—and quite frankly I don't feel any different about that now.

GS I remember Ken Reynolds used to fix my car. And Ken Reynolds was a wonderful guy. He really knew his job. And he would tell me confidentially that you couldn't really tell how much money a person had from how they dressed. And he had some of the musicians—who had more money than most people—as his customers, and he had learned the virtues of tolerance. He was an equal-opportunity grumbler.

His son married Susie and lives up on Ostrander Road, and he was on the cover of the *National Geographic* one year [for an article] about the Catskills. I looked at it and said—that's where my kids go to playschool—and I said, "How did you get that wonderful place?" And she said—and I'll never forget this—she said, "We were here first."

JW Susie?

GS Susie Reynolds. She also said—her information on the Onteora scene was—[that] it was very difficult to find a boyfriend because she was cousins to all of them.

BW This is a question to Michael. How much of an inspiration, for want of a better word, [were] Pan Copeland's activities to you? It seemed to me she was kind of a forerunner for that type of activity, and I wondered if she inspired or motivated you.

ML Well, the feeling of the Sound-Outs certainly influenced me . . . convinced me, if I had any doubt, that I wanted to do this in the country and in that kind of atmosphere.

BW Were there other activities like that throughout the country such as she had here, or was she kind of unique?

ML There weren't many of those. Concerts were in clubs and venues, and very few out in the field and country.

BW But for people who don't know about that, there was a field on, I guess it was her property, Glasco Turnpike and 212 . . . over

Annick du Charme and
Pan Copeland at the
Copeland Gallery
in August 1967.
Behind them is
Annick's painting
Chant Premier. Photo
courtesy of Ruth Drake.

Pan Copeland at
Ann's Delicatessen in
1967. Photo courtesy
of Tonny McNeil.

a rolling hill. She would have, I guess on weekends . . . maybe Fridays and Saturdays . . . she'd have bands in there playing, and my recollection is there were not more then several hundred people that would come. But it was kind of interesting. It was the first inkling I had [of] what that type of music was like and what that type of venue was like, and I just wondered if it was kind of an inspiration to you.

ML Yes, definitely.

BW She was a unique lady, I can tell you that. A feisty, feisty lady. One time I was escorting a candidate for the Senate. I was introducing him to shopkeepers and I said, "Pan, I'd like you to meet Jay Rolison." She said, "I don't want to talk to him, I want to talk to *you*." And with that she proceeded to climb up one side and down the other side about some issue in the town she had. She was that type of lady . . . very, very tough.

GS Jeremy, did you ever go to the Sound-Outs, or did your friends?

JW Oh, yes. I watched Tim Hardin fall off the stage at least half a dozen times.

GS Well, that doesn't include the Sled Hill [Café].

JW Tim managed to stand up at Sled Hill. Don't ask me how. Yes, we went to the Sound-Outs, and they were great.

GS Tim Hardin was one those absolutely wonderful musicians. It would be very hard for him to stay standing up, but then he'd play and there would be this incredible song. He was a beautiful, wonderful performer. He went right to your heart.

JW The town . . . the musicians that came here then . . . I mean, Ellen McIlwaine, whom I mentioned, was just a colossal singer.

Ellen McIlwaine (left) with **Pan Copeland**. McIlwaine was managed by Pan during her Polydor years, when she recorded *Honky Tonk Angel* and *We the People*. Pan drove her around the country to gigs in a Plymouth station wagon with a pushbutton transmission.
Photo courtesy of WoodstockArts Archives.

GS Fred Neil. Fred Neil was the same way.

JW Freddie Neil. Fred Neil didn't perform much. He didn't like to perform. Once in a while, after about his twelfth or fifteenth Irish coffee, he'd belt out one in the Sled Hill. But it was very, very rare when he would perform in public. And Van Morrison was living in town at the time, and he would play in the club that I worked in. Not that anybody remembers Jackie Lomax, but he had his North American debut here in Woodstock. The musicians that were here, of course, the ones that resided here for a long time . . . The Band, Butterfield, and Happy and Artie . . . played around an often lot. John Sebastian . . . they certainly added some depth and magic to the community . . . Somebody was saying, I believe it was you [gestures to Geddy]

Jeremy Wilber in front of the News Shop, fall 1965. (This is one of two photos circulated during the panel discussion.) Photo courtesy of Jeremy Wilber.

. . . I wonder what the next wave will be, because they certainly epitomized that one.

GS Did you know any of the other panelists here at that time?

JW Michael I knew. He was a customer of mine at the Sled Hill Café. And Jean of course. I remember Jean . . . I think prior to you, wasn't it Bill Reynolds's gun shop? The Juggler.

JY No, it was a place where [the owner] stored milk.

JW Was it? Oh, all right. I know at one point there was a gun shop in there.

GS Now, Bill West, he was certainly by no means the last Republican Supervisor . . . that honor may fall to you [nodding to Jeremy].

JW But Bill was a *registered* Republican.

GS Okay. So, when you were Supervisor . . . how did that era influence your role as Supervisor? I guess your constituency changed a lot . . . right?

JW I'm going to pass these around to people to look at to figure out what kind of character I was. Do you want to pass those around? They're contemporaneous photos of yours truly. At that time, the sixties, if nothing else there was a generational conflict. It certainly existed here in Woodstock. He [Bill West] was the establishment and we weren't. And the relationship was just very, very different. I didn't know Bill personally in those days at all.

BW You knew my son.

JW Yes, I knew your son. I went to school with Jeff.

BW You would come over to our house.

Jeremy Wilber poses with a bottle of Bellows Whiskey during his bartending days at the Sled Hill Café in 1969. (This is the other photo circulated during the panel discussion.) Photo courtesy of Jeremy Wilber.

Overview of Roots of '69 panel discussion. Photo by Julia Blelock.

JW Yes, I went to school with Jeff, but don't remember him. [laughter]

But, you know, it's interesting. There was something that I had overlooked at the time. But, again, we just thought it was all us versus them, kids versus grown-ups. And the constables in those days would spend all their time chasing us off the Green and chasing us out of the Artists Cemetery and any other place we wanted to hang out and do harmless things. And this was all perceived by us as a grievous injustice.

But *ABC News* came to Woodstock in 1971 to do a little human-interest piece on Woodstock. One of the people they interviewed was Mr. Varney of the bank, and something I didn't realize then . . . and talk about an establishment figure . . . was that he and his bank contributed what was then called the Longyear House to Family of Woodstock, and the whole purpose of that was to run this sort of informal social service agency for the kids who were flocking to the town, many of them without shoelaces, and this sort of gave them a blanket and a bowl of soup and whatever . . . and helped them to muddle on and muddle through.

But it was just so interesting watching that interview and seeing the real overt and sincere concern that the "establishment" at that time really had for the kids who were coming to town. At the time we—or at least I—perceived it very, very differently. We thought it was much more of an antagonistic relationship than it actually was.

Jean Gaede (from the audience) [unintelligible] . . . you know, Family [of Woodstock]. One girl would watch out for the kids. And when the fourteen-year-olds came to town she wouldn't turn them in to their parents and she wouldn't let the police know they were here until she had time to work with them and find out what kind of situation they were coming from. She was frantic. There was no place for them to camp or anything, so she put a telephone board in her house on Library Lane.

GS This was Gail Varsi, the red-headed woman . . .

Jean Gaede And the thing is, today Family is Ulster County's social services. So you see how it goes around. She came back here three years ago and I don't know what she thought . . . But it was a fantastic thing, and there are just certain people along the way who get totally forgotten, but she was really very big . . .

GS There were other people like that, people like Rush Harp and a bunch of others of us who started a bail fund for kids. And I'm going to tell you a story that I'm going to deny telling you afterwards. I was driving in my old red Dodge truck and Ludwig Baumgarten was following me and in his misguided view the truck was not driving straight. So he pulled me over and he [sharply asked for] "license and registration, please"—very official—and he looked at me and said, "Have you been smoking any drugs?" And clearly the

Paul McMahon speaks during the panel discussion. Photo by Dion Ogust.

answer yes would not be very good for me so I said, "No, Sir." And he said, "Let me smell." So I [gave him a quick exhale]. And he looked me right in the eye and said, "I can't tell." And that was his warning to me: You're local, you're okay, but please no smokin' drugs on the street.

Okay, onward.

Paul—last but not least—when did Woodstock hit your radar and when did you first come here?

Paul McMahon (PM) Well, I didn't move here until 1990, but I passed through here briefly in 1969 looking for the festival. I didn't see any signs and it really took quite a while for it to sink in that it was, like, sixty or seventy miles that way, you know. I think I bought a map. And I think things happen . . . I suspect that time doesn't really exist and so therefore you can look at the past and you can say, "Oh, so that's why that happened." Everything seems to happen for a reason, because time doesn't exist. But I did make it to the festival. I was kind of spoiled and a little on the wimpy side in those days, although I was a guitar player. I was nineteen and I was suffering mightily from the rain that was falling and my inadequate preparations for the weekend. The morning of Saturday there was an incident near me, and I don't know what really happened but at the time I thought that someone had been run over by a heavy, earth-moving piece of equipment. It happened very close to me. Then the next thing I heard was people talking about running out of water—"We're not going to have any water"—and I just freaked and so I—

Audience member People were told to stay away from the brown acid. Did you listen? Noooo.

PM I didn't have any brown acid. Anyway, as it turns out, my car was the very first car that was not parked in. The very last possible person who could have gotten out was me, and so I got out. I didn't attend it, but I came back here eventually, in 1990, on a spiritual search and have ended up being here. Really, it's a very special town for me. It's just the right place for me as far as I can tell. And I also note that Michael Esposito was supposed to play at the concert, backing up Tim Hardin, but he didn't think that Tim Hardin would be sober enough to make it there and so he didn't bother to go. So, meanwhile, a helicopter picked up Tim Hardin . . . and Michael ended up being a priest here.

GS And a bicycle repairman.

PM And a bicycle repairman, which is even more spiritual. I have family that lived here, but I was absolutely unaware of the scene here, completely unaware of it. And actually another turn happened in my life and I got completely out of music for the whole decade of the seventies. So if I would have ever found out about it . . . it just wasn't on my radar at all at the time.

GS Here's a spiritual golf ball I'll set up for you to hit.

PM All right.

Roskind's 2001 book.
Courtesy of Robert Roskind.

GS This book [Robert Roskind's *Memoirs of an Ex-Hippie: Seven Years in the Counterculture*] foretold that the Hopis would be conquered by the white man, but one day they would incarnate as white men themselves, wearing flowers and beads and being called hopis/hippies. Any thoughts?

PM I tried to find that book. I haven't been able to find it.

GS Robert Roskind.

PM I haven't tried very hard yet.

GS Okay.

PM But there are a lot of stories about Hopis. This might be true. I hadn't heard it before. It's a great idea and a lot of the stories that are supposed to come from Hopis that maybe don't are still often

Cover of 1989 **Woodstock School of Art** catalog. Block print by Robert Angeloch; used with his permission.

WOODSTOCK SCHOOL OF ART 1989

good ideas. I myself was on the Hopi reservation at one point and made a phone call to somebody and later heard my conversation with that person related back to me as a story of something that a Hopi elder told another elder. So, okay, there are a lot of Hopi stories.

GS   That is, Hopi, not hokey. What's your vision with the Mothership?

PM   Well, I really like a lot of the things I've heard here and I feel that Woodstock is a very important cultural Mecca. My grandfather was here in 1960 visiting Judson Smith. One of my uncles is Will Barnet, who was honored here at the Woodstock School of Art. And I feel that creativity and spirituality are very closely linked. I think it's a spiritual center and a creativity center, and I think it's multi-generational. I think it weaves different art forms, and so I also think that, I dimly suspect that, humanity might be at

Some of the **audience** for the Roots of '69 panel discussion.
Photo by Julia Blelock.

a little bit of a crossroads. I think . . . as far as I can tell, Woodstock is the most famous small town in America—in the world—and the most recognizable. And the town most closely associated with sex, drugs and rock 'n' roll . . . all good things. [laughter and applause] And, obviously, the key to the survival of humanity.

GS Great, so . . .

PM So that's what the Woodstock Mothership is about.

GS We're all convinced that Woodstock is a wonderful place and that, in a sense, some of its wonders are difficult to describe. It's also a delicate place—that is, you can't guarantee that these wonderful possibilities will happen, and you have to kind of participate yourself. You have to see it in others and encourage them. You have to kind of live in community life and we're all very lucky to be here. And so, I hope that there's a feeling not just of pride but a willingness to participate, as it says in the cemetery across the street, to contribute in your own way to the Woodstock way of life.

Audience Here, here. [applause]

GS So let me . . . before opening this to everybody's questions I want to just go around once more to review the question I was told to pose at the beginning of this discussion. How has the '69 festival influenced your thinking, and whether it makes you pessimistic or optimistic. Michael?

ML For me, very optimistic.

Audience member I guess it depends on how you define optimism.

ML Because it worked, and it was sort of a confirmation of our humanity, to me. The fact that people sort of rose to it, and gave the best of themselves, and took an immense amount from it. We came out of it—all of us who were there and a lot of the people who weren't—with a hope that we probably didn't have going in.

GS Jean?

JY Well, I think I was more a total optimist about change and what was going to happen. And I do remember asking Michael if he thought this was going to last and had any doubts about it. But I think you [Michael] were more a realist than I was about it. Being younger, it should have been the opposite way, but I remember that you said you thought that it could possibly go back and that there is no guarantee that this is going to go forward but it's a great experiment and it's something that can happen now. So Michael, I always thought, was very realistic about everything he did. And not as much as I was . . . very hopeful and very much thinking it was going to change things, that all of this was going to continue. And in many ways of course it is continuing. But of course the world as it is isn't how we hoped it would be.

GS It's interesting, you know, that some things will continue. In some ways it's hard to tell the foreman of the vessel sometimes, isn't it?
   Bill?

BW Well, I think I was deeply concerned about the way things were going at that time . . . I mean, it was very different for my contemporaries. And the community was changing rather dramatically. But I think what really happened—what happens through history—is that many of the good things from that particular event, and many of good things from previous and future events, meld themselves together and we move forward in a somewhat different way. But we each co-opt from the other, some good and some bad.

GS I've heard you talk about the county budget sometimes, and you express more optimism about this subject than that.

BW Do you want to discuss that now, Geddy? We have big problems.

JW I think there are as many potential problems with peace as there are with conflict. And the sixties was a time of course of great conflict. The social issues here at home—primarily the civil rights movement—and the Vietnam war. And it satisfies me that my generation made the statement that it did, both in peace and in conflict. So it doesn't make me necessarily optimistic or pessimistic. It satisfies me.

GS Paul?

PM Optimistic, chronically optimistic. Because I think when little good things happen, or sort of medium-sized good things happen, they have terrific ramifications for the future. So you have this mention of this one lady who was taking care of the fourteen-year-olds, and now you have this huge Family of Ulster County. And, you know, people have concerts in their yard and then you have half a million people in Bethel. I just want to say one thing, though, about the spirituality of this place. It's extremely ironic. There's an ironic spirituality that rules here. I think the Guru Rinpoche—the Tibetan—and the coyote are ascendant in Woodstock, and so you have the birth of a generation as a spiritual thing not unlike, say, the birth of Jesus or something like that . . . And it's in exactly the right place—the town is called Bethel, and that's forgotten; Woodstock is what's remembered. You know, coincidences and ironies. Anyway, I think I'm rambling.

GS Well, so I hear optimism. I hear kind of the idea that any optimism has within it, you know, seeds of unpredictability and sometimes tragedy, but that's the nature of optimism. You don't avoid it, because that could be true in some manifestation. And that Woodstock is a sophisticated enough place, and I think Karl Marx defines sophistication as the adulteration of commercial goods. That Woodstock is sophisticated enough that it can, you know, leaven the optimism and the sense of positivism about who we are and what we can do with a form of self-criticism and of belief in the discipline of hard work to obtain one's beliefs and, you know, the highest spiritual purposes people claim. Thank you very much, all. I'm going to open the floor to questions. I would ask you only not to make it too long, so the panel can respond, and I thank you very much for your attention. [applause]

Audience member I just saw, a few days ago, *Gimme Shelter*, which I didn't realize you had much to do with.

ML I didn't have much to do with it, but I was there.

Audience member Oh, you didn't produce it?

ML They had to move. They had to move their site a few days before the show.

Audience member Maybe with all that moving the question is not relevant. But that was so different from the Woodstock festival. You see the Woodstock film and then you see the racetrack and the Hells Angels beating the crap out of everybody. I was just so intrigued by it. It seems to be just the opposite of what was happening at Woodstock. It was so negative. I just wanted your comment.

ML It's preparation. There *was* none for Altamont. It came together really quickly . . . very little thought given to anything about what happens when the people get there. And let's bring the Hells Angels in for security. So it was sort of doomed.

GS Okay. Back there . . . hi, David.

David Boyle (from the audience) I came up in 1963. And since April 1964 I lived with Albert Grossman, Sally Grossman, Bob Dylan, Sara Lowndes, Victor Maymudes and Ramblin' Jack Elliott. Not being a music buff, but still enjoying a lot of music. There are some people who get short shrift around here. Albert Grossman was a great man. Paul Siebel was a balladeer unsurpassed. Many, many people were active and involved for a long time. Most of all, I feel short shrift goes to the natives of Woodstock who've been here a hundred and fifty years—no, try three hundred plus years. People who were so, so polite, were so skilled, were so able. They go way back, back to before 1900. They were so able . . . they were generous with their time, with their help, with many, many things. I think that there are remnants. There are people going back generations who are still here in the township. I don't think it can be discounted how many wonderful people are here from way, way back.

GS Comments?

Roots of '69 panel discussion. Photo by Julia Blelock.

PM That's something that I've noticed also . . . It's very rare that you have a community of conservative country people living shoulder-to-shoulder with the most radical artists and drug-crazed, sex-orgy musicians, and you have that going on for a hundred years in the same place as you have several generations of people who have grown up under those circumstances while still retaining their own identities. I think that's very important . . . a very well-woven community.

David Boyle Rather than just country people, we had people so skilled in so many trades and crafts, many involvements here . . . back to New York, up to Albany, all over. Their families still live here, please don't forget.

PM Oh, no, no. Those are the people who know how to skin a deer, dress a deer.

Audience member For Michael: The word "Woodstock" . . . who has the copyright of the Woodstock festival? What other terms and phrases? And how do you protect those?

ML It's basically the name of the festival that we have, as it pertains to music and festival-related things. I guess there are copyright infringements all the time and the ones that don't matter you don't bother with and the ones that do . . . you need to pursue or you lose your copyright.

Audience member Well, certainly, you've got a copyright on the Woodstock festival.

ML Yeah.

Alan Cohen (from the audience) I remember in 1963, when they had the March on Washington, [Walter] Cronkite was talking about it and he said the March on Washington was a success. There were two hundred and fifty thousand people there but in twenty years you'll find two million people who swear they were there. And I think Woodstock is very similar. I mean, I think people who think they were there weren't; they've seen the movie . . . so you probably had ten million people there.

GS There were also people there who think they weren't.

Alan Cohen Well, don't they say, "If you remember the sixties, you weren't there"?

GS The people here want to hear your witty questions, so they're going to link up a mike here so—I'm sorry . . . go ahead.

Alan Cohen Well, someone spoke who really knew the town well during the period immediately after the festival itself, in the early seventies when things changed very quickly up here. But it was the result of other things, probably, [not] just the festival, I think. The drug laws changed. The Nixonian period extended itself. Vietnam was getting ridiculous. Kent State. That was another nexus point, as [the Woodstock festival] was. It was getting really strange. So I think the festival timed itself to usher us into the seventies. I know Michael did other things before Woodstock, down in Miami. So it just was the perfect time. But it was a different time. I mean, [the] Woodstock of today is not that Woodstock, but it's a pretty nice place to live.

GS Got it. Any comments, folks?

JW Well, just on the ten million people who apparently went to the Woodstock festival. I was not one. I was here in Woodstock during the Woodstock festival. Tending bar, and seeing as much music as I was seeing, I didn't feel that I had to go and sit in the rain and watch it. But earlier it was mentioned how all these preparations were made to keep people out of Woodstock during the festival. I remember watching the proprietor of the Corner Cupboard stacking beer in his store. Cases and cases, up to the ceiling of his store, in anticipation of this big weekend. And he had that beer until the rest of the summer, because that was the deadest weekend. The only weekend that was nearly as dead as the weekend in 1969 was the weekend in 1994.

GS Was that Zane Zimmerman?

JW No, no, no. The Corner Cupboard, I think it was owned by Gene Meyer then.

Audience member With respect to the musicians and the spiritual search . . . I was thinking about a group of people, but they didn't really intersect. I know that Jimi Hendrix came to Woodstock to rehearse, and he rented a couple of houses, and he had this idea

Pan Copeland's business card for **Ann's Delicatessen** (renamed the Corner Cupboard in 1969). Courtesy of WoodstockArts Archives.

ANN'S DELICATESSEN

1 TINKER ST.

WOODSTOCK, N. Y.

PAN D. COPELAND   PHONE 67-9-9330

Ann's Delicatessen store account cards for **Jim Black** of the Mothers of Invention and **Julius Bruggeman**, site manager of the Woodstock Sound Festival. Courtesy of WoodstockArts Archives.

Billie ~~Monday~~ Mundie 1

Nov 1 – 1967 – ~~1004~~

~~110~~ eggs + grapes + forgot to charge

Nov 18 – ~~2.88~~ Phone Call 3.90

Dec 9 ~~3.12~~

~~.78~~

~~2.69~~

~~9.77~~

Jan 12 – 13.46

9.23

17.44

Jan 25 – 3.11   .42

"   27 – 7.31   1.10

"   29 – 9.61   .69

"   31   3.87 $.53

2.96   1.65

16.34

.64

Bob Dylan.

apr 14 – 1.00

Tim Hardin

Sept 3 – 20.49

Sept 4 –   6.26

" 5 –   13.10

~~" 6 –   10.00~~

Sept 8 –   6.17

" 8 –   2.66

" 8 –   1.90

" 16   4.78

" 16 –   4.98

" 19 –   2.69

Sept 19 – 2.16

Oct 11 – 7.91

"   15 – 3.94

"   15 – 7.78 cig 2

"   16   4.34

"   16 –   4.55   Dec 7 –

.45   4.00

$1.45

8.44

Dec 5   5.88

Ann's Delicatessen store account cards for **Billie Mundie** [sic], **Bob Dylan** and **Tim Hardin**. Courtesy of WoodstockArts Archives.

of a spiritual music growing out of this area. He called it "Sky Church," and then in fact he played that music he had rehearsed at Woodstock, and then subsequent to Woodstock. In later years, in the seventies and eighties, there was Karl Berger and the Creative Music Studio and people who had an interest both in music and [in] a spiritual expansion or expanded consciousness as part of the pursuit. Can you comment? I direct this to the entire panel. Do you have any anecdotes about Hendrix in Woodstock? And the same question about the Creative Music Studio.

JW I can tell you my Jimi Hendrix story. You know, it was very hard to be star-struck in Woodstock, because there were so many incredible people just walking up and down the streets in those years. He wasn't one of them. I mean, he was in the area, and Michael Jeffery, his manager, had a house, I think right around the corner here. But one day I was walking down the street by the Café Espresso and I happened to look in the window. And sitting at a table, looking at me the way I'm looking at you, with people around him—like people on this side of the table—was Jimi Hendrix. I have to say I was star-struck, and I just stopped and gawked a moment, and he went like this [gives a nod of recognition] and I moved on. You know, it's one thing that Woodstockers were very good at. I think that's why so many eminent people didn't mind hanging out here. We didn't gawk. The locals did not gawk. They did not fawn and did not chase after autographs. The last time I saw Bob Dylan was in the Sled Hill Café. I won't say he was a regular, but he wasn't a stranger either. But the last time I saw him, he came in—it was early evening and he was with Bobby Neuwirth and a couple of other guys—and they sat at a table and Dylan wanted to play a song. He wanted to play. We had Roger Tillison's guitar. It was kept in the storeroom . . . we never could trust Roger to take his guitar home with him. So somebody went and fetched Roger's guitar and gave it to Bob, and he was just putting the guitar on his knee and the door opened and these two young women walked in—never saw them before and never saw them since—and they saw Bob Dylan and they started to scream.

And he got up and he split and that was the last time I saw him. That was in 1970.

Audience member Did you hear any . . . was there any spiritual music?

JW Well, the spiritual music around at the time as I recall—and David mentioned Paul Siebel, and it's a spiritual experience listening to him. There was a group around then . . . and Spider is still around the town, Chrysalis, which I thought played very inspired and very transcendental music. And that's just to name some. There were a lot of groups, I think, that were very spiritual and transcendental in their taste.

GS I think attitude toward fame is an important part about Woodstock. I think Jeremy is dead right that if you live in an Entertainment Today world you gawk, you don't give people their space, you say, "Do you know where the Rolling Stones are rehearsing?" . . . Woodstock isn't like that. And it's really because everybody is entitled to their privacy, including people who are a part of the fame machine. I've never talked to you, Michael, really. We've talked a little bit over the years.

A Sound-Out performance check payable to **James "Spider" Barbour**'s Chrysallis [sic] band. Courtesy of WoodstockArts Archives.

ML Yeah.

GS We both moved to Wittenberg Road in 1968 and I haven't talked to him. We're about a mile and half apart. Maybe since the bridge is out we'll be talking now, I don't know.

Elliott Landy (from the audience) I missed some of this, but the town was basically founded by Caucasians who wanted to make a utopian society. And Michael coming here in 1968 or 1969 was really part of that process, and what he did culminated in or brought together all this spiritual energy, which was what Woodstock was founded in the first place for. I guess the festival was kind of an accident. Michael would be the first to agree with that. But there were all these spiritual intentions that everyone had. Michael saw what was happening and was part of it. It really manifested itself as a free festival and everyone thought, "Well, no one is going to make any money on this," but people have, over the years. So Woodstock is the result of a natural flow of events of the sixties and I write about it as more an example of what's possible than an example of what is. Because shortly thereafter we had the Altamont situation and everything went downhill. So we really see ourselves—all of us who were part of Woodstock—as part of that process [the manifestation of the possible]. And so the question is how to carry on with it. Everything was a surprise and everything was an accident [despite the fact that it] was all very well prepared for. But in the end it was a really cosmic event that happened, and created the flow of Woodstock.

GS [to **PM**] Any comment? I do notice the theme of spirituality keeps coming up again—different kinds of spirituality. You're a spirituality expert.

PM Well, I'd say that the idea of expanded consciousness goes hand-in-hand with the sixties: the drugs, especially psychedelics. If you look at the Beatles, the career of the Beatles—it's kind of the introduction of different drugs is a lot of what's going on. That's reflected in music, which is a perfectly malleable medium to carry a lot of complex ideas. Spiritual people are attracted to any sort of expansion of consciousness and that particular sort of potentiality of mind. So you have on that Sled Hill poster . . . one of the four acts is Swami Somebody I never heard of.

JW Swami Aumashananda. He was going to create the sound that created the universe.

Audience member What were the Sound-Outs like? Were there different musicians playing at the same time? Were there scheduled events and was there an artistic environment, or was everyone kind of hanging out? What was it like?

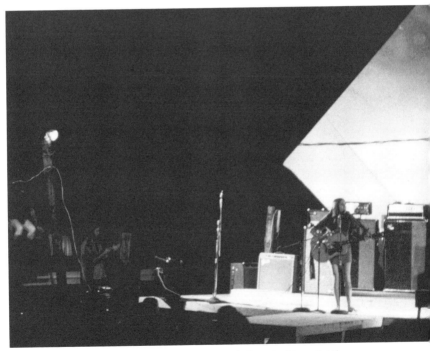

An unidentified folksinger performs at a **Sound-Out**. At this point the backdrop was still whole. Later on Wavy Gravy advised the promoters to cut "smiles" in the canvas to let the wind through. Photo courtesy of Bob Fass.

JW It had form. There were scheduled bands, there were posters, and there was a flatbed truck they used for a stage.

Daniel Eggink (from the audience) Because of the bird and the concept of spirituality, I wanted to ask Michael who . . . coined the phrase and decided to call it the first Aquarian Exposition. Because it had nothing to do with Woodstock when it started. It happened there, but who coined the term then? Because this is the spiritual link in the minds of millions. It was the first Aquarian Exposition.

ML I did. I came up with that.

Daniel Eggink May I ask you why?

ML Why? Because . . . there was a big spiritual component to what we were trying to do, and we wanted to tell people kind of what to expect and what we were trying to build here before they arrived. So, an Aquarian Exposition . . . something that would show off that spiritual side of our generation.

GS Thank you, Swami Lang. [laughter]

ML Pleasure.

GS Next—Jean.

Jean Gaede (from the audience) I want to speak of the fun, because in my life, when I talk about it, I always say, "Oh, I have had so much fun!" But my first neighbors were the Ballantines, and they had all the books and everything. They had an aunt called Emma Goldman, right? The house was mine to go into and get books and everything. Some of my later-on neighbors were Will and Ariel Durant. There were people with music. Wherever you talked or looked, you didn't know who was famous or who wasn't famous but everybody was doing exciting things, even the farmers. I wan-

Robin Williamson of the Incredible String Band at a Sound-Out show. Bob Fass knew Joe Boyd, the band's manager, and he booked the group for the festival. In 1969 the band played at the Woodstock Festival in Bethel. Photo courtesy of Bob Fass.

dered . . . I wandered . . . but I couldn't [leave] here, because it's so boring other places. I could mention in this room many, many names and you would all know who they were even though there would be no connection with me. They travel with us. And the spirituality for me was here in the mountains, to be able to see the mountains.

My grandfather would come in and say, "They're at it again." And my grandmother would say, "What is that?" And he would say, "They're painting that mountain again." But it *does* get you to look at it. And so, you know, it's been such a blast. I mean, everything and everybody.

People say to me, "And what do *you* do?" I say, "I applaud. What do you think I do? I applaud." It's been so much fun, right? [laughter and applause]

GS I think it's amazing. I'm wearing my James Joyce T-shirt here and *A Skeleton Key to Finnegans Wake* was written on Maverick Road by a couple of Woodstock guys. One was a professor at

Columbia and another a student there who became quite famous. It's really an intellectual community.

Audience member My question is for Michael Lang. The festival was actually an arts and music festival. How did you see the role of local artists in the festival, and when it moved to a different location how did that affect the role of local artists within the festival?

ML Well, we were local in several places along the way, so it's kind of hard to describe. But people who sort of came in to the event—artists who came in—stayed with us for the most part and moved with us. I brought a couple of people up from the University of Miami art department to oversee the art exhibits. We had some Native American art that we brought through a troupe of fifteen or sixteen people from New Mexico, and they put on a Native American art show. We had much bigger plans for the arts part of Woodstock when we originally started. But we had to rebuild a month before the show and we had to move and all that stuff happened. We just got the essentials done and the art just sort of came along with it.

JY You know, there was art at the time, which was all of the posters for musicians—the posters, the work. It was more or less [due to] Isaac Abrams, who lived here and still lives here. He was and really is one of the psychedelic artists, and he has been recognized as one of the few, very few, good psychedelic artists. And he was in the Whitney show represented by about, I think, four huge canvases that were incredible. But there was a lot of art that was design art and that was a part of the changing scene going back to Art Nouveau. And so those posters . . . and people were drawing all the time with ink and pens.

GS It's true. We don't want to diminish—

JY Do you remember that?

GS —[the fact] that Woodstock did remain an arts colony, a colony of artists, for a long time. Some of the artists were not quite of the caliber . . .

but then you think of someone like Milton Glaser, who's come up here every weekend for the last thirty years. And various others. It's a creative community. Publishing is one of the areas where it's still going. And spirituality. You know, I'm reminded today of that component of it, because I ain't no spiritual person but I think it does good things for people, so I'm really interested to hear about it . . . some of the things that I kind of haven't paid as much attention to as I should, for my salvation.

Audience member And that's exactly what I wanted to talk about . . . the spiritual component of it, which actually started at Monterey Pop as far as the gatherings go. The Eastern Mysticism was just as much a part of what my friends and I were into as the sex, drugs and rock 'n' roll, because a lot of people were going to India, a lot of people had read *Remember, Be Here Now*, a lot of people were hanging out with Ram Dass at Millbrook. And so I think people were learning how to meditate. I think there was a lot of that in addition to the art and the music. There was true spirituality budding in young people at the time, and it was prevalent in Woodstock and at the festival as well [as] with my friends.

PM I would agree with what somebody else said, that we tend to separate these things out as though they're separate concepts, but it was all one thing. This awakening in the sixties was spiritual, creative and social.

JW Well, I tell you, since you mentioned it and since the name Bud Sife has been mentioned . . . maybe this explains the idiosyncrasy he had of every Christmas Eve playing the *entire* Handel's *Messiah* in a café like the Sled Hill. That was interesting.

ML I was just going to say that Peter Max brought Swami Satchidananda to the festival. It was a very special moment for us and for everybody who was there. And he started the Integral Yoga movement in a really strong way and his comment was [that] the people in India would have been amazed to see something like this happening in America, which was such a materialistic society.

Franklin "Bud" Drake, *artiste extraordinaire* and proprietor of the Café Espresso. Photo by Ben Packer; courtesy of Ruth Drake.

OPPOSITE

Franklin "Bud" Drake's painting *Woodstock,* executed in 1998, makes reference to Ralph Whitehead and Hervey White, founders of the Byrdcliffe and Maverick colonies. Courtesy of Woodstock Artists Association and Museum.

It was interesting to hear that perspective from someone who was a totally spiritual person. There was a big spiritual component.

Richard Wronkowski (from the audience) One spirituality aspect that resulted from the Woodstock Music and Arts Fair, which I attended back in 1969: I still have the twenty-one dollars I was going to pay when I walked in there and no one took it.

ML You can leave it on the way out. [laughter and applause]

JY I knew you were going to say that.

Richard Wronkowski But the spirituality aspect . . . I've listened to what's happened here, and I know that I shared in that because I walked away from there . . . actually, we drove away on Sunday afternoon . . . with a sense of uplifted spirituality from the fact that we had had such a wonderful time in spite of the bad weather, in spite of the poor logistics and the traffic jams and all the other problems—I know everybody knows about that. It all came off so well. Everybody

had such a good time. It was a memorable experience. We knew we were a part of history, even then. But it wasn't until many years later that I was playing golf with Julius Bruggeman, who was one of the . . . instrumental people in the original Sound-Outs. And I had never been to a Sound-Out, never even been to Woodstock before I went to Bethel. I hadn't been to Woodstock actually until maybe ten years ago. But Julius, you know, he had a bad feeling about the whole thing because Rockefeller and the battle-lines people on the right passed their anti-drug laws. They're still on the books today. And the increased search-and-seizure laws happened, he feels, as a result of the bad taste in the mouth most of the establishment had about the way these hippies handled themselves.

I'm not trying to throw stones, but the spirituality thing probably would have happened anyway. But it would have been nice if that could have brought the battle lines closer together instead of dividing them more. But I wanted to mention Julius only because I didn't hear any mention at all of Franklin Drake, who was, I think, Pan's son. And he passed away about five years ago or something like that. And Jackson Frank, who was apparently a great musician and who was probably very instrumental in a lot of the Sound-Out activities, also passed away many years ago. I just wondered if anybody had any recollections of those people.

JW Yes, Jackson used to wash dishes at the Sled Hill. He was a poet. If he was the same Jackson Frank. Did he not experience a terrible fire?

Richard Wronkowski The story Julius told me is that he was burned in a potbelly-stove explosion in a wooden schoolhouse in Buffalo or Cheektowaga when he was a child. It was something like twenty years before the litigation finally panned out, and he got a fortune. Maybe it was fifteen [years]. It was a long time, anyway. And with this fortune he went to England and bought a Jaguar and befriended some of the musicians over there, a fair portion of their ilk, and Paul Simon, who was over there at the time. And indeed I think Paul Simon had something to do with making his last days more comfortable in an insane asylum here in the Woodstock area, as I recall.

PM He used to hang around at the Dharmaware Café in the early nineties.

Audience member My question is pretty much to the entire room. Spirituality—[unintelligible].

ML 2009? There might be. We're thinking about something.

Abigail Storm (from the audience) May I make a little comment on the spirituality issue? I just want to say that for many years one of the parts of the history of Woodstock has been suppressed. There are some active people that still are very concerned about the condition of our country and the rights of the people, and we have much information now that we didn't have before. Alternative culture is a group of people who actually have stood up and there-

This line drawing of the folksinger and writer **Jackson Frank** appeared in the *Woodstock Week* on February 15, 1968. Frank, originally from the Buffalo area, went to England and enjoyed some success as a folksinger there in 1965. For a time he wrote for the *Woodstock Week* and helped to promote the Sound-Outs and the local music scene through the newspaper. Courtesy of the *Woodstock Week*.

jackson frank

fore have been pushed to the fringe and been called radical fringe instead of the mainstream. Today, all of our forefathers would be called radical, as they were at that time, but what they did was they banded together and they stood up and defended themselves. They had to take up guns and establish something that we don't have to because it's already established, and that's the constitution of the states as well as the United States. We have to stand up if we believe that we are alternative, which I believe the Woodstock event was about. I mean, as far as what I heard about it, behind the scenes was very political, but a lot of that didn't get into the commercial venue. So one of the things that I tried to bring up to Michael, when they were putting on the twenty-fifth anniversary, was why weren't they doing it at the Woodstock site? Because the woman who owned the site was greedy, and I was a little concerned about that. We had also gone to John Roberts when we saw in 1990 that . . . in '89 . . . that there was a whole bunch of people that wanted to come together under the banner of peace and love and continue what was ended in the early seventies by Kent State. And it has only gotten worse. Our country has gotten worse, and this is what Woodstock is all about—I mean, the Woodstock event, its spiritual nature. If anybody is going to have another event called Woodstock, I would pray that they would be aware of the music, which was the primary element of Woodstock. And a lot of people would come, because as I tried to speak to Michael—

GS This is kind of long enough.

Abigail Storm Right, I just want to know.

GS I would like to give him a chance to respond.

Abigail Storm Let me make my final statement. Number one: Michael, have you ever considered having a free Woodstock event that would be funded by events through the year? And number two: have you considered the spiritual nature when you consider the bands and the music and the energy that would be put into the event?

ML Are you asking about a possible future event?

Abigail Storm I'm speaking about the fortieth anniversary. Right now there's a Web site. I don't know if it's yours, but it's on the Internet. It says "Woodstock.com under construction," and it shows a bandstand being built like the one in '69. So what's that about?

ML I'm not ready to talk about it.

Abigail Storm Okay, so that's why I asked the question.

GS We have to decide, as we pass through our lives, what's important, what we want to hold on to, what's worth giving our lives to. And that's a tough question. It's not always easy. But the one thing we do know is that as much as we celebrate the fortieth, the thir-

Lynn Miller and **Sredni Vollmer** perform at the contemporary Sound-Out. Vollmer was a long-time sideman of The Band's Rick Danko. He played harmonica with Danko beginning in the eighties. Photo by Julia Blelock.

tieth or the twentieth, what have you . . . we are right here now, and that's where we've got to start. And I think to be here now in Woodstock, to have had the opportunity to share thoughts about the past, is really a wonderful thing for this community. Because it enables us to answer the question of what should we be doing with our lives, what's important . . . better than we could before, so in that sense this free event has at least performed some function. Thank you! [applause]

Roots: A Photo Essay

Events Leading Up to the 1969 Woodstock Festival

Revelers at a **Maverick festival**. Photo courtesy of Woodstock Library.

The Social Harmonist, a hymnal, was compiled by **Lewis Edson Jr.** in 1800. Edson operated a sawmill in Mink Hollow (within the town of Woodstock) and supplied wood to the glass companies. Book cover courtesy of Woodstock Library.

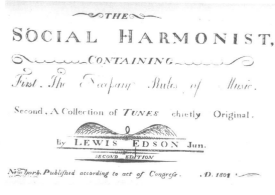

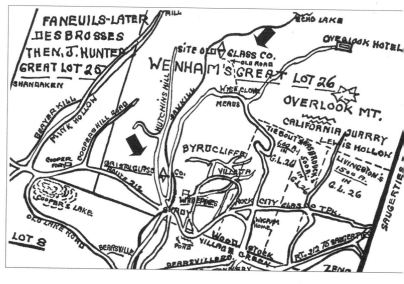

Detail of a map showing **Shady**, New York, a hamlet where five glass-making companies thrived in two separate locations over a span of nearly fifty years (see arrows). Beginning in 1809 with the launch of the Woodstock Glass Manufacturing Society and ending in 1855 when the last of the glassworks closed its doors, these firms constituted a vital economic engine for the Woodstock area. They produced not only utilitarian window and bottle glass, but also pitchers, decanters, candlesticks, bowls, domes and even canes and other "fancy" pieces. An early and financially viable example of the Arts and Crafts movement in Woodstock. Map by Anita M. Smith; courtesy of WoodstockArts Archives.

Glass canes from the glass-making era. Courtesy of WoodstockArts Archives.

Dan Sully in one of his Woodstock fields. Sully was an important figure in American theatre in the late 1800s. He wrote and produced a string of plays, including *The Corner Grocery*, 1884; *Daddy Nolan*, 1885; *Capital Prize*, 1886; and *Old Mill Stream*, 1903. In 1886 he married Louisa Fox, whose mother had been born in Mink Hollow, Woodstock. He and his bride purchased a summer place in Mink Hollow. Here, Sully took up farming and rehearsed his theater companies. His play *Old Mill Stream* was set in Woodstock. Postcard courtesy of Historical Society of Woodstock.

The **Villetta Inn**, one of more than thirty buildings making up Woodstock's Byrdcliffe Arts and Crafts colony. The colony was founded in 1902 by Ralph Radcliffe Whitehead, a visionary and arts patron, Hervey White, a writer, and Bolton Brown, an art professor and lithographer. Whitehead possessed the wherewithal to fund a utopian colony—a select group of people gathered in a beautiful setting to create esthetically pleasing handmade objects. The idea was to challenge the mechanistic factory age by reviving the ancient handicrafts of weaving, iron work, furniture making and pottery in a place that was healthful for the mind as well as the body. Though the enterprise as launched by Whitehead never made much money, the campus survived, and today is prospering under the auspices of the Woodstock Byrdcliffe Guild.
Photo courtesy of the Byrdcliffe Collection of the Woodstock Byrdcliffe Guild.

BYRDCLIFFE ARTS & CRAFTS

WOODSTOCK, ULSTER CO., N. Y.

Checks payable to R. Radcliffe-Whitehead

DECORATED FURNITURE ✦ METAL WORK ✦ HAND WOVEN CURTAINS AND RUGS ✦ ✦

FOLK-SONGS
OF
EASTERN EUROPE

EDITED BY
RALPH RADCLIFFE WHITEHEAD

BOSTON
OLIVER DITSON COMPANY
New York   Chicago
CHAS. H. DITSON & CO.   LYON & HEALY

Detail of **Ralph Radcliffe Whitehead's** Byrdcliffe letterhead. Courtesy of the Byrdcliffe Collection of the Woodstock Byrdcliffe Guild.

A collection of songs edited by **Whitehead** in 1912. He translated many of the original verses into English. Title page courtesy of New York State Library.

Hervey White, the co-founder (with Fritz Van der Loo) of the Maverick, a music and art colony just over the Woodstock town line in West Hurley. In 1916 White held the first of the Maverick festivals, to defray the costs of an artesian well. The violinist Gabriel Peyre and a handful of other musicians played Tchaikovsky, directed by Leon Barzin Sr.
Photo courtesy of Historical Society of Woodstock.

A **Maverick festival crowd** waiting for the evening's performance
to begin. The orchestra pit can be glimpsed at the left, near the
front of the stage. The first Maverick festival proved so successful
financially that White continued to produce the festival through
1931. At the height of its popularity, upwards of eight thousand
people attended. Each year a new theme was announced. One
August the Maverick celebrated a gypsy carnival. Another season
Walter Steinhilber presented *The Pirate Ship*. Other years featured
Farrell Pelly's *Circus* and a fantasy from *1001 Arabian Nights*,
Scheherazade. Admission was reduced for attendees who took note of
the theme and dressed accordingly. Photo courtesy of Woodstock Library.

Audience for the **Maverick Concert Hall's** inaugural performance in 1916. The building was constructed by Hervey White and helpers, with wood harvested from the nearby forest. Today this hall hosts the oldest continuously running summer chamber festival in the United States. Photo courtesy of Historical Society of Woodstock.

THE MAVERICK SUNDAY CONCERTS
Begin June 14, at 4 o'clock

Resident artists for 1925 are...
Georges Barrere, (flute)
Reber Johnson, (violin)
Edwin Bachmann, ,,
Armand Combel, ,,
Paul Lemay, (viola)
Henri Michaux, ,,
Horace Britt, (cello)
Engelbert Roentgen, ,,
Inez Carroll, (piano)
H. Rovinsky, ,,
Visiting artists will occasionally assist.
Season tickets for 12 concerts (ending Aug. 30,) are $6.
Single admissions, 75 cts.
Send subscriptions to Hervey White, Woodstock. N. Y.

Program announcement for June 14, 1925, mailed to Miss Wilna Hervey, among other Woodstockers. Miss Hervey was a star of the silent screen. In *The Toonerville Trolley* (a series based on a popular comic strip), she played The Powerful Katrinka. Program courtesy of Historical Society of Woodstock.

OPPOSITE

The violinist **William Kroll** was a frequent performer at the Maverick. The photograph is inscribed, "To the Van der Loos." Fritz Van der Loo co-founded the Maverick music and art colony with Hervey White. Photo courtesy of Historical Society of Woodstock.

Barbara Moncure, daughter of the painter Joseph Pollet and stepdaughter of the artist Rolph Scarlett, grew up during the thirties in Canada, California and Woodstock. With folksinger and local historian Harry Siemsen she recorded *Folksongs of the Catskills* for Folkways in 1963. She is pictured singing with her daughter Judi, age six, in Woodstock's Magic Meadow circa 1962. This is one of a series of photos taken for the Folkways album cover. Photo by Alf Evers; courtesy of Judi Bachrach.

Mendel Levy, **Eugene Ginsberg**, Beat poet **Allen Ginsberg**, **Naomi Ginsberg** and **Louis Ginsberg** in a (circa) 1936 family photo. The group had come to Woodstock to visit poet acquaintances. In a 1955 letter to Eugene Brooks the poet mused about his family's Woodstock summer cottage and the old swimming hole.[1] It has been suggested that the house was located some five blocks from town. Edward Sanders, a close friend of Ginsberg's, a fellow Beat poet and a Woodstock resident, thinks that it may have been sited on lower Ohayo Mountain Road near Sully's Bridge (close to the current Woodstock Inn on the Millstream).[2] © Allen Ginsberg / CORBIS.

[1] Letter to Brooks: Bill Morgan (Ed.), *The Letters of Allen Ginsberg* (Philadelphia: Da Capo Press, 2008), p. 119.

[2] Barry Miles, *Ginsberg: A Biography* (London: Virgin, 2000), p. 18. E-mail from Edward Sanders to Weston Blelock, January 15, 2009.

The **Cheats and Swings**, a square dancing group organized by
Dyrus and Edith Cook for the town's sesquicentennial in 1937.
The group became so polished that they were invited to dance for
President and Mrs. Roosevelt on August 27, 1938, at Hyde Park,
New York.[3] The dancers are, clockwise from top: Harvey Fite,
Mary Boggs Soles, Craig Vosburgh, an unidentified woman and
man, Towar Boggs and an unidentified woman. In the center is
May Boggs. The musicians are, from left: Bill Allen, Walter Shultis
and Percy Hill. They are pictured here at the Colony Arts Center
in Woodstock. Photo courtesy of Historical Society of Woodstock.

[3] "Cheats-Swings Will Dance for Pres. Roosevelt," *The Overlook*, Vol. 6, No. 15
(August 19, 1938), p. 1.

Camp Woodland, Phoenicia, New York: Pete Seeger at the annual end-of-summer folk festival, circa 1947. John Herald, a bluegrass musician and member of the Greenbriar Boys, saw Seeger at one such appearance in 1954 and later said that it inspired him to become a musician. The purpose of Camp Woodland, founded in 1940 by Norman Studer, among others, was to involve young campers in local history, folklore and the folk life of the Catskill Mountains. Photo courtesy of Norman Studer Papers, M. E. Grenander Department of Special Collections and Archives, University at Albany Libraries.

In 1942 **Henry Cowell**, "the father of twentieth-century American music," purchased a house in Shady, a hamlet of Woodstock. Cowell was a music pioneer and a prolific composer, and he numbered George Gershwin and John Cage among his students. Cowell is pictured here in Berlin, circa 1930, playing his Irish walking tune-cum-clusters called "Exultation." Photo courtesy of Music Division, New York Public Library for the Performing Arts; Astor, Lenox and Tilden Foundations.

Sam Eskin, a folksinger and folklorist, and **Sonia Malkine**, a clear-voiced French folksinger. Sam arrived in Woodstock in 1948 and Sonia moved to town in 1953 with her husband—the French Surrealist painter Georges Malkine—and family. This photo was taken circa 1962 in front of Sam Eskin's house on Chimney Road, Woodstock. Photo from Estate of David Gahr; courtesy of Sonia Malkine.

The acclaimed painter, silkscreen printer and folksinger **Bernard Steffen** at an August 1958 concert presented at the Polari Gallery. This was Sonia Malkine's debut performance. Photo courtesy of Sonia Malkine.

Polari Gallery flyer for a show featuring the stellar banjo player Billy Faier. That same year (1958) Faier was the featured banjo player for the hit Broadway musical *The Unsinkable Molly Brown,* and he soon had three albums out—two on the Riverside label and the third on Elektra. In 1959 Faier appeared at the Newport Folk Festival. Courtesy of Fern Malkine-Falvey Archives.

POLARI GALLERY
presents
BILLY FAIER

IN A
CONCERT
OF SONGS

WITH

5 STRING BANJO
AND GUITAR

Admission
$1.50   including tax

Saturday, Sept.13, 8:40 pm

POLARI GALLERY is located on Chestnut Hill Road, first right past the golf course off Rt. 212, Woodstock, N.Y.

Pan Copeland, "mother of the Woodstock Festival of 1969," behind the counter at Ann's Delicatessen in 1958. In the early sixties students from SUNY New Paltz visiting Woodstock made a beeline to Pan's deli for her great sandwiches. In the mid-sixties Pan opened the Copeland Gallery and in 1967 she hosted a series of Sound-Out concerts on her eight-acre farm just over the town line in West Saugerties. Musical acts such as the Colwell-Winfield Blues Band, Fear Itself, Tim Hardin and John Herald performed at these concerts. Photo courtesy of Ruth Drake.

Jim Hamilton and **Franklin "Bud" Drake** opened the Café Espresso in 1959. The Parisian-style bistro provided an inviting rendezvous for artists, musicians and writers. Both Hamilton and Drake were graduates of the Pennsylvania Academy of the Fine Arts. An early musical performer at the Espresso was Peter Yarrow of Peter, Paul and Mary fame. In 1962 Bernard and Mary Lou Paturel purchased the venue and brought Billy Faier in to book the acts. Photo courtesy of the *Ulster County Townsman*.

Diners on the terrace of the **Café Espresso** in 1959.
Sonia Malkine is the waitress at right. Photo by Earle
Fichte; courtesy of Fern Malkine-Falvey Archives.

ORiole 9-9346.

COLONY ARTS CENTER

ROCK CITY ROAD   One Block From Post Office

WOODSTOCK, N. Y.

JULY 31 — AUG 1   ADM $1.50

FIRST ANNUAL

CATSKILL

MOUNTAIN

FOLK MUSIC FESTIVAL

WOODSTOCK, NEW YORK — Participants range from 75 year old Mary Avery to 7 year old Judith Moncure, from "Bearded Bill" Spanhake, fiddler and humorist, to young Billy Faier, folk singer and banjo virtuoso.

In between are Sam Eskin, nationally famous as singer, guitarist and folk song authority; French-born singer and lute player, Sonia Malkine; Harry Siemson, fire-chief and Catkaill Mountain folk-loreist; Barbara Moncure, noted for her singing and collecton of Hudson Valley and Catskill Mountain folk songs; Bernard Steffan, artist and folk singer; story teller and singer "Squire" Elwyn Davis of Shokan. Entire program will be Mo'd by Alf Evers, writer, historian and president of Woodstock Historical Society.
THIS EVENT IS SPONSORED BY THE WOODSTOCK HUDSON CHAMPLAIN CELEBRATION COMMITTEE

Flyer for the **First Annual Catskill Mountain Folk Music Festival**, summer 1959. Courtesy of Fern Malkine-Falvey Archives.

Pictured at Sam Eskin's house on Chimney Road in 1960 are, from left: **Sonia Malkine**, **Bernard Steffen**, **Lou Gordon**, **Sam Eskin**, **Billy Faier** and **Ruth Wolfert**. Photo courtesy of Fern Malkine-Falvey Archives.

Woodstock Chamber of Commerce summer booklet for 1960. Beginning in the late fifties the program guide was titled *The Woodstock Festival* and featured a bird on the cover, designed by Ed Chavez. Courtesy of WoodstockArts Archives.

Woodstock Playhouse
WOODSTOCK, N. Y.

PRESENTS

Concert

TOM
PAXTON
TOM
PAXTON
TOM
PAXTON

TUES.AUG.6

8:40 p.m.   All Seats $2.75
For Information and Reservations
Call (914) 679-2015

Concert poster for a show featuring the world-renowned folksinger **Tom Paxton** at the Woodstock Playhouse. Edgar Rosenblum, a theatrical producer, art gallery owner and music promoter, purchased the playhouse in 1959. Since 1957 he had been offering concerts at the Polari Gallery on Chestnut Hill Road. In 1961 musical acts were booked in addition to summer stock theatre fare. By 1962 special midnight concerts were being offered, and in August of that year Pete Seeger appeared before an enthusiastic standing-room-only crowd. Courtesy of Historical Society of Woodstock.

First Annual Woodstock Folk Festival official program guide. The festival took place September 14 to 16, 1962. According to Sonia Malkine, Pete Seeger donated concert receipts from his Woodstock Playhouse appearance to fund part of the festival. Front cover of the guide courtesy of Historical Society of Woodstock.

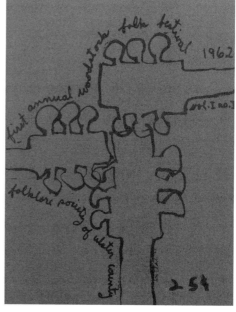

Five of the eight Folk Festival event founders, from left: **Sonia Malkine**, **Sam Eskin**, **Mona Fletcher**, **Frank Fletcher**, **Bill Hoffman**. Not pictured are Bill Deutsch, Eleanor Walden and Billy Faier. Headliners at the festival included the founders plus Pete Seeger, Barbara Moncure and Harry Siemsen. Photo courtesy of Sonia Malkine.

OPPOSITE

Bob Dylan. "The White Room" was a studio upstairs from the Café Espresso where Dylan worked (in 1964) on the albums *Another Side of Bob Dylan* and *Bringing It All Back Home.* Mary Lou and Bernard Paturel, the owners of the Espresso at that time, gave Bob the use of the space and he thanked them in the liner notes for *Another Side of Bob Dylan.* Dylan told Mary Lou that he had trouble sleeping and she often heard his typewriter tap-tapping away at two and three o'clock in the morning. This was one of the most productive periods of his career.[4] Photo by Douglas R. Gilbert.

[4] Mary Lou Paturel. Interview by Weston Blelock, December 11, 2008.

Pictured from left are: *Candy* co-author **Mason Hoffenberg, John Sebastian**, a co-founder of the Lovin' Spoonful who had a top-ten Billboard Hot 100 hit with "Do You Believe in Magic" in 1965, **Bob Dylan**, and Dylan's roadie, **Victor Maymudes.** Photo by Douglas R. Gilbert.

Edward Chavez, a sensitive artist whose abstract work captured the canyons and intricate rock formations of the Southwest, arrived in town from Colorado in 1945. He learned to play guitar from Spanish-American hoboes in his youth. In 1963 Bob Dylan began dropping by Chavez's Plochmann Lane home seeking feedback on songs he was working on, such as "Blowin' in the Wind." He never arrived any later than eleven thirty at night as Chavez and his wife had a small child who needed her sleep.[5] Photo courtesy of Eva Van Rijn.

[5] Eva Van Rijn. Interview by Weston Blelock, November 21, 2008.

Sled Hill Café. Bud Sife founded this storied venue as a coffee shop in 1964. In 1967 a macrobiotic menu was offered and the venue styled itself as the Woodstock Paradox Restaurant, after an eatery of the same name in New York City. The restaurant's manager was John "Jocko" Moffitt, a Californian who had arrived in town the year before. Those pictured in the front row include the cook (at left) and Jocko's young son Eric (center). Behind them are Jocko's daughter Jenny; Joan Morgan, a family friend; Bob Dacey, the salad-prep man (seated), who was also a member of USCO, the media art collective; and Jocko. The following year the venue was transformed into a nightclub where musicians like Paul Butterfield and Van Morrison hung out and jammed. Photo by Peter Kahn; courtesy of Tonny McNeil. The photo embellishments are Tonny's.

Bob Dylan with his manager, **Albert Grossman**, a formidable and savvy music veteran who was adept at spotting authentic talent. In 1962 Grossman signed Bob Dylan to his roster and in 1963 he moved to Woodstock. Soon Dylan came to stay at his home on Striebel Road. Initially Grossman loved Bob like a son,[6] but later they parted on bitter terms. Grossman's stable over the years included acts such as Odetta, Richie Havens, Paul Butterfield, The Band, Janis Joplin, Gordon Lightfoot, Electric Flag, and Peter, Paul and Mary. ©BarryFeinsteinPhotography.com.

[6] Joel Gilbert, *Bob Dylan World Tours: 1966–1974 / Through the Camera of Barry Feinstein* (Oaks, Pa.: MVD Visual, 2005).

Jazz Festival Coming To Woodstock?

THE RECORD PRESS

Representing All The News In WOODSTOCK, TOWN OF OLIVE, ONTEORA CENTRAL SCHOOL DISTRICT.

Vol 8, No. 53 Two Sections   WOODSTOCK, N.Y.   WEDNESDAY, DECEMBER 30, 1964   TEN CENTS

Jazz Would Bring 1000s

An earlier announcement that the world famed and always tumultuous Newport Jazz Festival was interested in moving its location to Woodstock in 1965 has been greeted with enthusiasm by many, viewed with dismay by others. There is not doubt that the Festival is superb enter-

Interesting statistics in light of the fact that Wein sees Woodstock capable of handling only 6,000 jazz fans at the most. Although the Newport license only called for 12.000 patrons. the park there usually bulged at the seams with 14,000, including more than a thousand standees. The

Woodstock Jazz Festival. George Wein, the Newport Jazz Festival impresario, sought to transplant the Newport festival to the Woodstock area via the Woodstock Estates—which was the site of the First Annual Woodstock Folk Festival in 1962. Headlines courtesy of the *Record Press*.

Ad in the *Woodstock Week* of August 18, 1966. **The Juggler**, opened that year, was owned and operated by Jim and Jean Young. It offered avant-garde books and art and music supplies. In 1968 Michael Lang, the promoter of the 1969 Woodstock Festival, befriended the Youngs and they in turn became early supporters of his vision for the '69 festival. Courtesy of the *Woodstock Week*.

Bill Militello, an industrial and product designer, was also the proprietor of the Woodstock Motel. He is pictured here with a school bus that he modified and drove on trips around the United States. Albert Grossman was a good friend and put up numerous rock clients at the motel. Photo courtesy of Denice Militello.

OPPOSITE

John Herald, of the Greenbriar Boys, met **Kim Chalmers**, a Woodstock native, at the Café Espresso in the summer of 1965—at the owner's family table. The atmosphere at the venue was free and easy. The musicians and patrons mingled and relaxed together in those early days—as the art colony transitioned into a rock music scene. A year later John and Kim were married. They are shown here at a picnic in 1967.[7] Photo by Happy Traum; courtesy of Kim Herald.

[7] Kim Herald. Interview by Weston Blelock, December 22, 2008.

When they first arrived in Woodstock in 1967, **Rick Danko** and his fellow musicians stayed at the Woodstock Motel. Rick struck up a friendship with Bill Militello, who told him that a place was available for rent in West Saugerties.[8] This was "Big Pink," and the group that would become known as The Band began working informally there with Bob Dylan. *The Basement Tapes* grew out of these sessions. Pictured on Easter Sunday 1968 are, from left, **Levon Helm**, **Garth Hudson**, **Richard Manuel**, **Robbie Robertson** and Rick Danko. Photo by Elliott Landy.

[8] Bill Militello: Levon Helm with Stephen Davis, *This Wheel's on Fire: Levon Helm and the Story of The Band* (Chicago: Chicago Review Press, 2000), p. 150.

OPPOSITE

In 1963 **Peter Walker**, a folk instrumentalist, organized a seventy-two-hour hootenanny in Boston that raised $35,000 for a children's hospital. Headliners included Karen Dalton, Tim Hardin and the Holy Modal Rounders. Bob Dacey invited Peter up to Woodstock in 1966 to check out the swimming holes. Peter is a big swimming fan, but he was not impressed with Big Deep, a revered local spot.[9] Photo courtesy of Peter Walker.

[9] Peter Walker. Interview by Weston Blelock, December 20, 2008.

INTERMEDIA

212
212

painting, happenings, sculpture, dance, poetry, karate, events, expanded theatre, filmmaking, electronic music etc. R. Liikala, Coordinator, Group 212, Box 96, Woodstock, N.Y. 12498
tel. 914-CH 6-8287

SUMMER WORKSHOP • JUNE 15 • SEPT 15

Ad in a local newspaper for **Group 212's Intermedia Workshop**. The workshop was set up in 1967 by John "Bob" Liikala at the old Holiday Country Inn and Resort, just over five miles from the Woodstock Village Green along Route 212. Although no formal music program was offered, in 1967 the workshop hosted a number of concerts by such musical acts as The Cyrkle ("Red Rubber Ball"), Don Preston, keyboardist for the Mothers of Invention, and Juma Sultan, best known as Jimi Hendrix's conga player for Gypsy Sun and Rainbows. Bob Liikala's compound was located not far from "Big Pink" and he recalls hearing The Band's practice sessions through the woods. Courtesy of John Liikala Archives.

John "Jocko" Moffitt in 1966. Moffitt, a drummer and a carpenter, came to Woodstock with the idea of producing an outdoor festival. He had seen a number of folk festivals in his native California. As Peter Walker tells it, Jocko heard from his girlfriend, Sunshine, about Peter's marathon hoots, and button-holed him during the summer of 1967 in New York City's Central Park. Moffitt organized the first Sound-Out on Labor Day weekend on Pan Copeland's farm over the Woodstock town line in West Saugerties, New York. The *Woodstock Week* reported an attendance figure of two thousand. The performers included Richie Havens, Tim Hardin, Junior Wells, Billy Batson and Major Wiley. Stephanie Marco, Richie Havens's girlfriend, remembers arriving at the field in the band's van on a late summer afternoon and hearing the incredible drumming. "It was a time of innocence, she recalls, "and everybody was gathered around the music."[10] Photo courtesy of Tonny McNeil.

[10] Stephanie Marco. Interview by Weston Blelock, January 9, 2009.

Billy Batson, a performer at the Labor Day 1967 Sound-Out, seen here at the Café Espresso circa 1966. Photo courtesy of Tonny McNeil.

Major Wiley was a performer at a number of the Sound-Outs, including the Labor Day 1967 event. Photo courtesy of Eric Devin.

The March 31, 1968, **Sound-Out** was the last festival event under the stewardship of John Moffitt. Jerry Moore, a Freedom Rider, befriended Richie Havens in Greenwich Village.[11] By 1964 he had been signed by John Hammond to a Columbia Records contract. Soon afterwards he arrived in Woodstock and performed at the Café Espresso when Major Wiley bowed out of an engagement. On March 31, 1968, he appeared on the bill with his old friends Richie Havens and Major Wiley. (Wiley's name is misspelled on the poster.) Moore notes that it took a while for the townspeople and the musicians to get comfortable with each other. One day Paul Butterfield was walking along Tinker Street, says Moore, and a car pulled up beside him. When Butterfield glanced inside the car he noticed that Billy Waterous, the town constable, was motioning for him to get in. Butterfield did so, but with some trepidation. The car sped off to a distant point in the country and finally pulled up to a house. The twosome went inside and found musical instruments laid out in the living room. Eventually someone ambled over and asked Paul to help him identify a chord on his guitar. That was the extent of the "police action."[12] Poster courtesy of Historical Society of Woodstock.

[11] Don Moore. Interview by Weston Blelock, January 13, 2009.

[12] Jerry Moore. Interview by Weston Blelock, February 13, 2009.

Richie Havens performing at the March 31, 1968, Sound-Out, which took place at the Woodstock Playhouse. This show marked Jocko Moffitt's final involvement with the Sound-Outs. Photo courtesy of Eric Devin.

Pan Copeland's business card signals the next incarnation of the **Sound-Out**. In 1968 the event became known as the Woodstock Sound Festival. Pan Copeland bankrolled the event, tapping James Matteson to handle advertising and accommodations. Jackson Frank was brought in as the talent booker and Pan hired Julius Bruggeman as the events manager.[13] Courtesy of WoodstockArts Archives.

[13] Julius Bruggeman. Interview by Weston Blelock, November 23, 2008.

OPPOSITE

Julius Bruggeman circa 1968. Julius recalls that when Pan Copeland arrived at the field she was received with "pomp and circumstance." Pan's Sound-Out vision was to establish an annual "Newport Rock Festival." And it was Julius Bruggeman, not Jackson Frank, who ended up booking the talent. Julius approached the Blues Magoos, the Colwell-Winfield Blues Band and Tim Hardin and offered them the going rate of fifty dollars. Charlie Chin, the banjo player for Cat Mother and the All Night Newsboys, noted the informal booking policy. He suggests that bands of his acquaintance were invited to play for food and board. Bruggeman says that Bob Dylan and Albert Grossman were frequently backstage and he estimates that one particular weekend featured no fewer than seventy-three musical acts. Occasionally Jimi Hendrix and his manager, Michael Jeffery, were also at the field.[14] Photo courtesy of Julius Bruggeman.

[14] Julius Bruggeman. Interview by Weston Blelock, November 23, 2008.
Charlie Chin. Interview by Weston Blelock, February 13, 2009.

THE VILLAGE VOICE
SHERIDAN SQUARE   PHONE WA 4-7880
NEW YORK, NEW YORK 10014

1417

DATE *June 28* 19 *68*

RECEIVED FROM *Sound Festival*

THE SUM OF *Fifty Eight and* $\frac{80}{100}$ DOLLARS $ *58* $\frac{80}{}$

FOR *ad for 7/4/66*

AMOUNT OF ACCOUNT $_____
AMOUNT PAID . . . . $_____   *Thank You!*
BALANCE DUE . . . . $_____   BY *Pat Vestal*
☐ CASH   ☐ CHECK   ☐ M.O.

Receipt dated June 28, 1968, regarding an ad placed in the **Village Voice**. (Notes associated with this receipt refer to Jackson Frank, Secretary of the Woodstock Sound Festival.) Courtesy of Ruth Drake.

A **Sound Festival legal form** that includes Pansy Copeland, President, Jules Broggerman [sic], Vice-President, and James Matteson, Treasurer—and signals the dissolution of the partnership. Courtesy of Ruth Drake.

CERTIFICATE OF DISSOLUTION OF

Sound Festival, Woodstock, N.Y., Inc.

Under Section 1003 of the Business Corporation Law

We, the undersigned, the holders of ~~all~~ *two thirds of the* outstanding shares entitled to vote on a dissolution of the corporation, hereby certify:

1. The name of the corporation is *Sound Festival, Woodstock, N.Y., Inc.*

2. Its certificate of incorporation was filed by the Department of State on *July 5, 1968* under the name *Sound Festival, Woodstock, N.Y., Inc.*

3. The name and address of each of its officers and directors are:

DIRECTORS

NAME   ADDRESS
Pansy Copeland
Jules Broggerman
James Matteson

OFFICERS

NAME   ADDRESS
President - Pansy Copeland
Vice-President - Jules Broggerman
Treasurer - James Matteson

Woodstock Playhouse
WOODSTOCK, N. Y.
PRESENTS
Monday Music Festival
HAPPY &
ARTIE
TRAUM
★ ★ ★ ★ ★ ★ ★
MON. 14 8:30 P.M.
JULY ALL SEATS $3.00
For Reservations Call (914) 679-2015

Happy Traum, a singer, songwriter and guitarist, performed at the Café Espresso in the spring of 1963. He was with the New World Singers at the time, but appeared solo on that gig. The group broke up in 1964 and in 1966 Traum and his family spent the summer in Bearsville. It was at this point that he renewed his friendship with Bob Dylan, whom he had first met in 1961 in Greenwich Village. By 1967 Traum had moved here permanently. His younger brother, **Artie**, soon followed. By this time the brothers had teamed up as a premier folk singing duo, performing at such venues as the **Woodstock Playhouse**. In 1968 the pair appeared at the Newport Folk Festival, the Philadelphia Folk Festival and the Woodstock Sound Festival.[15] Poster courtesy of Historical Society of Woodstock.

[15] Roger Dietz, "Artie Traum: Changing Partners, Changing Times," *Sing Out!* Vol. 44, No. 1 (1999), p. 3 (available online: http://www.singout.org/artietraum.pdf). Michael Gray, *The Bob Dylan Encyclopedia* (New York: Continuum, 2006), p. 668–69. Happy Traum. Interview by Weston Blelock, February 16, 2009.

Radio personality **Kip Carson** (Mike Gordon) of Poughkeepsie's
WKIP circa 1968. Carson was engaged to publicize and emcee the
events of July 4 and July 19. He arrived at his first show to a sight he
"will never forget." There were three or four state troopers with their
cars, as well as assorted sheriff's deputies and local cops standing
around unsure what to do—while across a stone wall some three to
four hundred people were gathered on blankets "making out" and
passing around wineskins and joints. Kip Carson was used to civic
and school events, but this was something completely different. As he
walked through the entrance a young girl in a sundress approached
him and offered him corn on the cob. One of the bands that Kip
recalls fondly was the Blues Magoos. Their hit "(We Ain't Got) Nothin'
Yet" peaked at number five on the Billboard chart in the United
States and they had opened nationally in 1967 for The Who and
Herman's Hermits. Kip remembers them alighting from their truck
and setting up in under twenty minutes. Their performance was very
tight and had a recording-studio quality. Odetta performed several
exotic African folksongs, and the crowd loved them. Then Richie
Havens did an impressive twenty-five-minute version of "Freedom."
Kip muses that Havens must have had "fingers of steel, due to
his insistent and fast strumming."[16] Photo courtesy of Mike Gordon.

[16] Mike Gordon. Interview by Weston Blelock, February 14, 2009.

A pair of **Sound-Out tickets** for July 20, 1968. Around that time Pan Copeland turned to a new group of individuals to run the festivals. This team, Coyote Productions, included Bob Fass, Cyril Caster and Pan herself.[17] Scott Fagan, one of the performers, took his wife, Patricia, to the July 20 performance. Fresh from St. Thomas, U.S. Virgin Islands, Patricia was struck by the energy that surged through the crowd, and she envied the nude people for their freedom and sense of connectedness to the land.[18] One time in Pan's field, Ellen McIlwaine and others from Fear Itself lay on their backs looking up at the stars. Much to their astonishment they saw six large points of light moving in tandem across the sky.[19] Flying saucers? Sketches of UFOs made their way into subsequent Sound-Out posters. Courtesy of WoodstockArts Archives.

[17] Cyril Caster. Interview by Weston Blelock, January 31, 2009.

[18] Patricia Fagan. Interview by Weston Blelock, February 8, 2009.

[19] Ellen McIlwaine. Interview by Weston Blelock, November 30, 2008.

Open Air

SOUND FESTIVAL

Copeland Farm

SATURDAY, JULY 20, 1968

Starting at 3:00 p.m. — Continuous thru Evening

N⁰ 1261   Admission $3.00

Open Air

SOUND FESTIVAL

Copeland Farm

SATURDAY, JULY 20, 1968

· Starting at 3:00 p.m. — Continuous thru Evening

N⁰ 1262   Admission $3.00

Woodstock Sound Festival poster for August 16 and 17, 1968. Chris Zaloom, lead guitarist for Fear Itself, recalls piling off the Trailways bus with his wife, Carol, and fellow band members, and making his way over to Pan Copeland's deli to sort out a ride. When the town constable got ready to sweep them along, Pan came sailing out her door and said, "You children, get over here." After that the law moved on. During the Sound-Out, Ellen McIlwaine, the band's leader, played keening guitar solos. Mustafa, the Zalooms' black dog, jumped on stage and howled along in back-up support. Larry Packer of Cat Mother and the All Night Newsboys recalls that Ellen's performance was "Janis Joplin-like." Ellen says that soon after the show Jocko Moffitt became their road manager. She describes him as a "salt of the earth," very resourceful and capable type. One time as Jocko was driving with the band back from Chicago, the radiator sprang a leak. He added red pepper. That took care of the leak, but the car smelled like soup all the way back to Woodstock. Courtesy of Chris Zaloom.

The Woodstock Week

Henry Crowdog's **Rosebud Sioux** at the August 16, 1968, show. Photo from the *Woodstock Week.*

Another shot of Henry Crowdog's **Rosebud Sioux**. According to Bob Fass, it was raining and Henry promised to stop the rain by the end of his act so the show could go on. Photo courtesy of Bob Fass.

Woodstock Sound Festival poster from late summer 1968. In the spring of 1968 Cat Mother and the All Night Newsboys rented a farmhouse from Pan Copeland for ninety dollars a month. They later discovered that it was haunted—hence the low rent. When they moved in they found crucifixes in lipstick and red nail polish adorning some of the walls. Since the band had no money they decided to make it their home base, despite all. That summer they became the Sound Festival's host band.[20] Folksinger Scott Fagan remembers stopping by the house with his wife, Patricia, to visit his friend Roy Michaels, the band's bassist. He was introduced to the other members of the band and also met many lovely ladies and assorted earth mamas. He was "a stranger in a strange land." After performing his song "The Greatest Love," Scott felt the setting was appropriate and the timing magical. He says there was a warm connection between the performers and the audience. Bob Fass, host of *Radio Unnameable* on WBAI, emceed this event. He adds that while he helped to book some of the bands, profit was in the background—people were there for the music. According to Cyril Caster, in 1968 WBAI was like today's NPR. It had cred and clout. When Bob Fass promoted the Woodstock Sound Festivals on the air he provided real push. Larry Packer says that this Sound-Out "was the very first festival I attended. I'm glad it was that one. There was an awakening going on." Courtesy of Christine Anderson.

[20] Charlie Chin. Interview by Weston Blelock, February 13, 2009.

Bob Fass, the Woodstock Sound Festival emcee, exits the stage after introducing Peter Walker. Photo courtesy of Bob Fass.

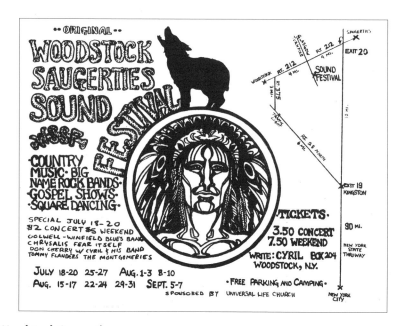

Woodstock Saugerties Sound Festival poster for 1969. An ambitious schedule of eight different festivals was planned that year. James "Spider" Barbour, guitarist for Chrysalis, played shows in 1968 and again in 1969. He recalls that the Sound-Outs prior to 1969 went very smoothly but that the '69 events were plagued by rainy and chilly weather. Rain, according to event promoter Cyril Caster, was very much a problem, and as a result few events were successfully staged. Courtesy of Cyril Caster.

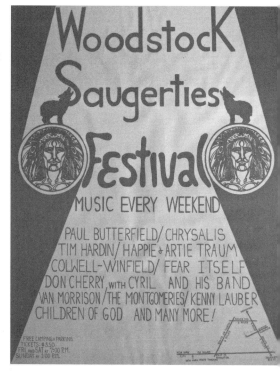

Sound-Out performance check made out to Van Morrison. When he rented a house on Ohayo Mountain Road, Morrison was new in town and had not yet scouted out the music scene. The owner suggested he contact Cyril Caster, who recommended that Morrison audition members of the Colwell-Winfield Blues Band.[21] Van Morrison relates in Brian Hinton's *Celtic Crossroads* that he had seen members of the Colwell-Winfield Blues Band previously, in Boston. When the band moved to Woodstock it was breaking up, and he recruited some of the musicians for his *Moondance* album.[22] It is known that Colwell-Winfield alumni such as Jack Shroer and Collin Tilton did receive credits on *Moondance*, one of Van Morrison's best-known albums. Courtesy of Ruth Drake.

[21] Cyril Caster. Interview by Weston Blelock, January 31, 2009.

[22] Brian Hinton, *Celtic Crossroads: The Art of Van Morrison* (London: Sanctuary Publishing, 1997), p. 104.

OPPOSITE

Woodstock Saugerties Sound Festival poster for 1969. Headliners included Paul Butterfield and Van Morrison. The poster artist was Blaine Saunders. According to Cyril Caster, Blaine sketched the Indian chief and the coyote freehand but drew inspiration for the coyote from a Flying Burrito Brothers album cover. Cyril says that one reason why the Woodstock Music and Arts Fair (in 1969 at Bethel) did not have the word "festival" in its moniker is that it was already in use with the Woodstock Sound Festival. Courtesy of Happy Traum.

Ed Sanders, a member of The Fugs, backstage with **Janis Joplin** in New York City on February 17, 1968. This was at the Anderson Theater during one of Joplin's first New York shows. A friend of Janis's, Ed had always tried to visit her "whenever she played, in New York or in California."[23] Beginning in the spring of 1968, he urged her to break with Big Brother and the Holding Company. Later that year she did so.[24] Photo by Elliott Landy.

[23] E-mail correspondence from Edward Sanders to Weston Blelock, February 20, 2009.

[24] Edward Sanders, *1968: A History in Verse* (Santa Rosa, Calif.: Black Sparrow Press, 1997), p. 232.

WOODSTOCK MUSIC & ART FAIR
presents
AN AQUARIAN EXPOSITION
in
WHITE LAKE, N.Y.*

3 DAYS of PEACE & MUSIC

WITH

Joan Baez	Keef Hartley	The Band
Arlo Guthrie	Canned Heat	Jeff Beck Group
Tim Hardin	Creedence Clearwater	Blood, Sweat and Tears
Richie Havens	Grateful Dead	Joe Cocker
Incredible String Band	Janis Joplin	Crosby, Stills and Nash
Ravi Shankar	Jefferson Airplane	Jimi Hendrix
Sly And The Family Stone	Mountain	Iron Butterfly
Bert Sommer	Quill	Ten Years After
Sweetwater	Santana	Johnny Winter
	The Who	

FRI. AUG. 15   **SAT. AUG. 16**   **SUN. AUG. 17**

All programs subject to change without notice
*White Lake, Town of Bethel, Sullivan County, N.Y.

A **Woodstock Festival brochure** picked up in 1969 by Weston Blelock at Hapiglop, a leather shop in Woodstock. Courtesy of WoodstockArts Archives.

Woodstock **constabulary** instruction notice for the local switchboard. Courtesy of Historical Society of Woodstock.

CONSTABLES:

    THE FOLLOWING INFORMATION TO BE USED WHEN ANSWERING CALLS PERTAINING TO THE WOODSTOCK ART AND MUSIC SHOW:

    THERE IS NO MUSIC FESTIVAL TO BE HELD IN WOODSTOCK, CONTRARY TO SOME REPORTS.

    THE SO-CALLED "WOODSTOCK MUSIC AND ART FAIR" HAS BEEN SCHEDULED AT <u>WALL KILL</u>, ORANGE COUNTY, NEW YORK, FOR AUGUST 15, 16 and 17th.

    THIS AREA IS REACHED FROM ROUTE 17 OR THE "QUICKWAY".

    WRITE TO WOODSTOCK MUSIC, PO BOX 996, RADIO CITY STATION, NEW YORK.

    RADIO REPORTS INDICATE THIS AFFAIR HAS BEEN DENIED PERMISSION BY THE WALLKILL TOWN AUTHORITIES.

    WE SUGGEST YOU CONSULT YOUR NEWSPAPER OR WALLKILL OFFICIALS BEFORE PROCEEDING FURTHER.

Gilles Malkine, son of the French folksinger Sonia Malkine, in a New York City studio with Tim Hardin and album producer Gary Klein (backs to camera) in 1969. They were working on the album *Bird on a Wire*. Gilles appeared with Tim at the 1969 Woodstock Festival. Photo by Voy Stark; courtesy of Sonia Malkine.

OPPOSITE

Aerial view of The Villager, the **Woodstock Motel** (top center) and the Methodist church. The church was purchased by Bill Militello and his wife, Hilde, in 1967 and converted into the **Tinker Street Cinema**. Sy Kattelson, a *Glamour* photographer, signed on as projectionist and manager. The theater featured Militello's Austin three-manual, fifteen-rank theater organ, complete with toy counter, chimes, drums and marimba. The organ had four thousand pipes and weighed twelve tons. At one time it had belonged to the Paramount Theater in Newark, New Jersey. Bill hoped musicians would rent the hall for concerts.[25] On August 10, 1969, Juma Sultan booked a midnight concert there. The opening act was the Aborigine Music Society, followed by Jimi Hendrix with the Gypsy Sun and Rainbows. (Hendrix was tuning up his band for the Woodstock event in Bethel a week later.) About fifty people attended, and the concert became known as the Tinker Street Jam.[26] Photo by Henry DeWolf; courtesy of Denice Militello.

25 "Church Faces Changes," *Woodstock Week*, Vol. 16, No. 3 (April 20, 1967), p. 2. "Tinker Street Cinema Preparations," *Woodstock Week*, Vol. 3, No. 46 (November 22, 1967), p. 1. Roberta Militello. Interview by Weston Blelock, January 31, 2009. Denice Militello. Interview by Weston Blelock, February 3, 2009.

26 Steven Roby, *Black Gold: The Lost Archives of Jimi Hendrix* (New York: Billboard Books, 2002), p. 132.

Backmatter

The August 9, 2008, Sound-Out featuring the group **Naked**: Tony Lee Thomas on guitar; Kevin Past, bass; Rachel Marco Havens, vocals; Julia Nichols, vocals; Johnny Watson, drums; and Di Cross, vocals and violin. Photo by Julia Blelock.

Questions Prepared for the August 9, 2008, Panel Discussion

For Michael Lang

• After the success of the Miami Pop Festival, what drew you to Woodstock?

• Describe the Woodstock you found.

• How did festivals like the Maverick and the Sound-Outs inspire and guide your thinking?

• Who was Peter Goodrich and what impact did he have?

• When did you meet Jim Young and why did you put him on retainer?

• Who were some of your first musical contacts in the community?

• How did your ideas about founding a recording studio evolve, and why didn't you pursue this project post-festival?

• Did you meet Albert Grossman at that time? Did he provide any support or advice?

• Who was Alexander Tapooz?

• There has been much speculation about how the name of the festival was chosen. Supposedly Michael Foreman (in charge of the 1969 festival program guide) and Stanley Goldstein (the festival's headhunter and campground coordinator) said the name had to "convey a sense of freedom, of both thought and physical presence." You are said to have replied, "We gotta keep the name Woodstock. It really has a mystical feeling about it." Please comment.

For Bill West

• How did you first hear about the 1969 Woodstock festival event?

• Can you describe the thinking about/attitude toward the proposal at the local political level?

• What were some of the concerns?

• In the late 1960s the *Ulster County Townsman* carried numerous articles on the so-called hippie problem—regarding loitering, law and order, narcotics, health and sewer issues, and recreational camping. Are there any related anecdotes you can share? For example, did you attend the non-partisan meeting on hippies convened by Mrs. Peggy Egan on June 22, 1969?

• As a county official, were you called up to Tapooz's?

• Can you recall what transpired after that?

For Jean Young

• You arrived in Woodstock in 1966 from Berkeley, California. Can you compare what you found in Woodstock vis-à-vis California—artistically, intellectually and musically?

• Why did you found The Juggler and how did the community respond?

• Did you and Jim attend any Group 212 events? Was this a Maverick-like organization?

• Do you recall meeting John "Jocko" Moffitt? What sort of fellow was he?

• Did you attend any of the Sound-Outs? If so, can you describe what that experience was like? Did you attend any with Michael?

• In 1979 you and Michael co-wrote a book titled *Woodstock Festival Remembered*. Do you recall if Michael mentioned how the early Woodstock festivals might have influenced his thinking?

For Jeremy Wilber

• As you were growing up in Woodstock, what impact did the influx of musicians have on you?

• Can you offer some anecdotal information about how Woodstock changed in 1967, 1968, and 1969 and then post-festival—from your vantage point at the Sled Hill Café?

• Did you ever attend a Sound-Out? If so, what was your take?

• Did you meet any of the other panelists at that time?

• How did that era influence your later role as Town Supervisor?

For Paul McMahon

• When did Woodstock hit your radar?

• When did you first arrive here?

• Robert Roskind, in his book *Memoirs of an Ex-Hippie: Seven Years in the Counterculture*, writes about an ancient Hopi prophecy. It foretells that the Hopis will be conquered by the white man but will one day incarnate as white men themselves—wearing flowers and beads and being called hopis/hippies. Any thoughts?

• There are many sixties themes extant in Woodstock. Which ones have you embraced, and why?

• What is your vision with regard to the Mothership?

For all the participants

• How did the 1969 festival influence your thinking? Did it make you hopeful or depressed?

• How does that era manifest itself in your life today?

• Will there ever be another event like the 1969 festival?

• If there is such an event, what will be the circumstances?

About the Panelists

Michael Lang came to Woodstock in 1968 to stage the Woodstock Festival of 1969. As head of the Michael Lang Organization he produces and manages live events. Among the musicians he has represented are Joe Cocker and Rickie Lee Jones. Current projects include a book of memoirs, *The Road to Woodstock*, being published in 2009.

Jean Young arrived in Woodstock in 1963 via Berkeley, California, and New York City. She had studied art with her mentor and friend Judith Rothschild and also with Hans Hoffmann, the Abstract Expressionist master. She continues to paint today. In 1966, together with her husband, Jim Young, she founded The Juggler, a book, art and music store in Woodstock. She went on to write the *Woodstock Craftsman's Manual* in 1971 (second edition, 1973) and to co-author a number of books with her husband. In 1979 she wrote *Woodstock Festival Remembered* with Michael Lang.

Bill West is a lifelong resident of Woodstock and a principal of William E. West, Inc., a construction and real estate development company. From the early 1960s to the present he has ably represented Woodstockers as a Town board member and Supervisor, county legislator and, most recently, the town's Republican Party chair.

Jeremy Wilber arrived in town in 1952. He is a playwright, builder, master bartender and four-time Town Supervisor. During the late sixties he tended bar at the legendary Sled Hill Café. He is currently at work on a novel about the sixties decade, tentatively titled *Endymion in Woodstock*.

Paul McMahon came to Woodstock in 1969 to attend the festival and returned here to live in 1990. His musical lifestyle is emblematic of the sixties in motion. In addition to his music he is the creative force behind the Woodstock Mothership, a gallery, nightclub and healing center.

Geddy Sveikauskas, the moderator, publishes the *Woodstock Times* as well as three other papers and is the owner of Ulster Publishing.

Sound-Out of August 9, 2008

Program

Weston Blelock, Executive Producer
Paul McMahon, Producer
Justin Foy, Emcee
Rabbi Joshua Yisroel, Opening Benediction

Performers

(in order of appearance)

Hair of the Dog
Peter Walker
Spiv
Jeremy Bernstein
Steve Knight
Joey Eppard
Frankie and His Fingers
Norman Wennet
Mighty Xee
Marian Tortorella
Paul McMahon
Dharma Bums
Tim Moore
Justin Love
Lynn Miller and Sredni Vollmer
Naked
Nathaniel

Paul McMahon performing at
the contemporary Sound-Out.
Photo by Julia Blelock.

Sources

Books and Articles

Deitz, Roger. "Artie Traum: Changing Partners, Changing Times." *Sing Out!* Vol. 44, No. 1, 1999.

Evers, Alf. *Woodstock: History of an American Town*. New York: Overlook Press, 1987.

Gray, Michael. *The Bob Dylan Encyclopedia*. New York: Continuum, 2006.

Helm, Levon, with Stephen Davis. *This Wheel's on Fire: Levon Helm and the Story of The Band*, 2nd ed. Chicago: Chicago Review Press, 2000.

Heppner, Richard, Ed. *Woodstock Years*, Vol. 2. Woodstock, N.Y.: Publications of the Historical Society of Woodstock, 2007.

Hinton, Brian. *Celtic Crossroads: The Art of Van Morrison*. London: Sanctuary Publishing, 1997.

Miles, Barry. *Ginsberg: A Biography*. London: Virgin, 2000.

Morgan, Bill, Ed. *The Letters of Allen Ginsberg*. Philadelphia: Da Capo Press, 2008.

Roby, Steven. *Black Gold: The Lost Archives of Jimi Hendrix*. New York: Billboard Books, 2002.

Roskind, Robert. *Memoirs of an Ex-Hippie: Seven Years in the Counterculture*. Blowing Rock, N.C.: One Love Press, 2001.

Sanders, Edward. *1968: A History in Verse*. Santa Rosa, Calif.: Black Sparrow Press, 1997.

Smith, Anita M. *Woodstock History and Hearsay*. Woodstock, N.Y.: WoodstockArts, 2006.

Spitz, Robert Stephen. *Barefoot in Babylon: The Creation of the Woodstock Musical Festival, 1969*. New York: Viking Press, 1979.

Studer, Norman. *A Catskill Woodsman: Mike Todd's Story*. Fleischmanns, N.Y.: Purple Mountain Press, 1988.

Young, Jean, and Michael Lang. *Woodstock Festival Remembered*. New York: Ballantine Books, 1979.

Film/Video/DVD

Gilbert, Joel. *Bob Dylan World Tours: 1966–1974 / Through the Camera of Barry Feinstein*. Documentary, 120 mins. Oaks, Pa.: MVD Visual, 2005.

Newspapers

Catskill Mountain Star, Saugerties, N.Y. Published weekly as the *Catskill Mountain Star* from 1927; as the *Saugerties Post Star* from June 1, 1971, to April 18, 1972; as the *Old Dutch Post Star* from April 25, 1972, to November 6, 1994; as the *Sunday Old Dutch Post Star* from November 13, 1994, to December 3, 1995; as the *Old Dutch Post Star* from December 10, 1995, to January 28, 1996; and as the *Saugerties Post Star* from February 3, 1996, to the present.

Kingston Daily Freeman, Kingston, N.Y. Published as the *Rondout Daily Freeman* for five months in 1871; as the *Daily Freeman* from 1872 to October 26, 1878; as the *Kingston Daily Freeman* from October 28, 1878, through December 1969; and as the *Daily Freeman* from January 1970 to the present.

The Overlook, Woodstock, N.Y. Published weekly from 1933 to 1941, when the name was changed to the *Woodstock Press.*

Woodstock Record Press, Woodstock, N.Y. Published weekly as the *Woodstock Press* from November 1953. It became the *Woodstock Press and Onteora Record* in the late 1950s; the *Record Press* in April 1963, and the *Woodstock Record Press* on March 2, 1966. The paper ceased publication in 1967.

Ulster County Townsman, Woodstock, N.Y. Published weekly as the *Woodstock Townsman* from 1953 and as the *Ulster County Townsman* from 1955 to the present.

Woodstock Times, Woodstock, N.Y. Published bi-monthly from February 7, 1972, through May 25, 1972, and weekly from June 1, 1972, to the present. (On January 4, 2001, the editorial offices moved from Woodstock to Kingston, N.Y.)

Woodstock Press (formerly *The Overlook*), Woodstock, N.Y. Published weekly in 1941/42.

Woodstock Week, Woodstock, N.Y. Published weekly from May 15, 1964, to July 2, 1964, and from 1965 to September 19, 1968.

Interviews

Barbour, James "Spider," January 15, 2009.
Bruggeman, Julius, November 23, 2008.
Caster, Cyril, January 31, 2009.
Chin, Charlie, February 13, 2009.

Drake, Ruth, November 21, 2008.

Esposito, Michael, December 18, 2009.

Fagan, Patricia, February 8, 2009.

Fagan, Scott, February 6, 2009.

Faier, Billy, November 17, 2008.

Fass, Bob, January 15, 2009.

Gordon, Mike (radio name Kip Carson), February 14, 2009.

Herald, Kim, December 22, 2008.

Liikala, John "Bob," December 8, 2008.

Malkine, Sonia, December 14, 2008.

Marco, Stephanie, January 9, 2009.

McIlwaine, Ellen, November 30, 2008.

McNeil, Florence "Tonny," January 12, 2009.

Militello, Denice, February 3, 2009.

Militello, Roberta, January 31, 2009.

Moncure, Peter, November 17, 2008.

Moore, Don, January 13, 2009.

Moore, Jerry, February 13, 2009.

Packer, Larry, February 2, 2009.

Paturel, Mary Lou, December 11, 2008.

Pollet, Elizabeth, January 8, 2009.

Rosenblum, Edgar, November 21, 2008.

Sife, Bud, November 17, 2008.

Steffen, Ellie, November 17, 2008.

Stern, Gerd, February 2, 2009.

Sultan, Juma, February 17, 2009.

Traum, Happy, February 16, 2009.

Turner, Rob, December 19, 2008.

Van Rijn, Eva, November 21, 2008.

Walker, Peter, December 20, 2008.

Wapner, Jerry, January 31, 2009.

Yalkut, Jud, January 28, 2009.

Young, Jean, December 12, 2008.

Zaloom, Carol, September 4, 2008.

Zaloom, Chris, September 4, 2008.

Acknowledgments

This project was born of a panel discussion held on August 9, 2008, at the Colony Café in Woodstock. We would like to thank the participants, most notably Michael Lang, Jean Young, Bill West, Jeremy Wilber, Paul McMahon, Geddy Sveikauskas, and audience members Jean Gaede, Elliott Landy, David Boyle, Alan Cohen, Richard Wronkowski, Abigail Storm and Daniel Eggink. Without their contributions the project would not have evolved into this book. We would also like to thank the event's sponsors: the Historical Society of Woodstock and the Woodstock Chamber of Commerce and Arts.

D. J. Stern, Amy Raff and Thomas Whigham of the Woodstock Library proved unfailingly helpful with the book. Carla Smith of the Woodstock Byrdcliffe Guild, JoAnn Margolis of the Historical Society of Woodstock, Emily Jones of the Woodstock Artists Association and Museum, and Paula Nelson of the Woodstock School of Art assisted us as well. Other institutions that were very supportive include the Saugerties and Kingston libraries and the Howard Greenberg Gallery. Joseph Geller of the Green Library at Stanford University kindly responded to our inquiries about Allen Ginsberg.

We are extremely grateful to the following for their time and support: Christine Anderson, Judi Bachrach, James "Spider" Barbour, Julius Bruggeman, Charlie Chin, Eric Devin, Ruth Drake, Michael Esposito, Patricia Fagan, Scott Fagan, Billy Faier, Bob Fass, Jean Gaede, Mike Gordon, Rachel Marco Havens, Kim Herald, Elliott Landy, John "Bob" Liikala, Gilles Malkine, Sonia Malkine, Fern Malkine-Falvey, Stephanie Marco, Ellen McIlwaine, Florence "Tonny" McNeil, Denice Militello, Roberta Militello,

Peter Moncure, Don Moore, Jerry Moore, Larry Packer, Mary Lou Paturel, Elizabeth Pollet, Edgar Rosenblum, Pete Seeger, Bud Sife, Letitia Smith, Ellie Steffen, Gerd Stern, Juma Sultan, Happy Traum, Rob Turner, Eva Van Rijn, Peter Walker, Jerry Wapner, Jud Yalkut, Toni Weidenbacher, Jean Young, Carol Zaloom and Chris Zaloom. We would like to thank three people who helped on countless occasions with research questions: Edward Sanders pinpointed salient research on Allen Ginsberg; Paul McMahon helped to run down key facts, furnished us with telephone numbers and supported the project in numerous other ways; and Cyril Caster patiently provided supporting details on the sixties era.

Thanks go also to our splendid copy editor, Jane Broderick, and our wonderful book designer, Abigail Sturges.

Any errors or omissions in the book are our own. We apologize for any inconsistencies or oversights.

About the Editors

Weston Blelock grew up in Woodstock and received his early education at the Gordonstoun School in Scotland. During summer vacations he enjoyed several of the Sound-Outs, and he also attended the Woodstock Festival of 1969. He later produced and hosted a syndicated radio show in Canada. After returning to Woodstock in 1999, he undertook, among other projects, a second edition of Anita M. Smith's *Woodstock History and Hearsay*. This award-winning "art edition" was published by WoodstockArts in 2006. He is a principal of WoodstockArts and Vice President of the Historical Society of Woodstock.

Julia Blelock also grew up in Woodstock. Her parents prohibited her from attending the 1969 festival in Bethel, promising that she could "go next year." Recovering from this major disappointment, she began a publishing career in Manhattan, later switching to the field of information technology. In 1999, after living and working for many years in New York and Los Angeles, she too returned to Woodstock. Here, she has continued her sales and marketing activities in the high-tech sector and has worked locally on cultural tourism initiatives. She has returned to her publishing roots with WoodstockArts.

Index

Page numbers in *italics* refer to illustrations.